Gabriele D'Annunzio

Twayne's World Authors Series
Italian Literature

Anthony Oldcorn, Editor

Brown University

TWAS 805

GABRIELE D'ANNUNZIO
Photograph courtesy of Il Vittoriale degli Italiani

Gabriele D'Annunzio

By Charles Klopp

The Ohio State University

Twayne Publishers
A Division of G. K. Hall & Co. • *Boston*

Gabriele D'Annunzio
Charles Klopp

Copyright 1988 by G. K. Hall & Co.
All rights reserved.
Published by Twayne Publishers
A Division of G. K. Hall & Co.
70 Lincoln Street
Boston, Massachusetts 02111

Copyediting supervised by Barbara Sutton.
Book production by Gabrielle B. McDonald.
Book design by Barbara Anderson.

Typeset in 11 pt. Garamond
by Williams Press, Inc., Albany, New York.

Printed on permanent/durable acid-free paper
and bound in the United States of America.

Library of Congress Cataloging-in-Publication Data

Klopp, Charles.
    Gabriele D'Annunzio / by Charles Klopp.
       p.   cm.—(Twayne's world authors series; TWAS 805. Italian
    literature)
    Bibliography: p.
    Includes index.
    ISBN 0-8057-8243-5 (alk. paper)
    1. D'Annunzio, Gabriele, 1863-1938—Criticism and interpretation.
I. Title. II. Series: Twayne's world authors series; TWAS 805.
III. Series: Twayne's world authors series. Italian literature.
PQ4804.K55   1988
858'.809—dc19   88-12385
                                                                        CIP

Contents

About the Author

Charles Klopp has degrees from Princeton and Harvard universities. He has taught at Robert College in Istanbul, and at Harvard, Stanford, Princeton, and Ohio State. In addition to work on D'Annunzio, he has written on Petrarch, Ariosto, Tasso, Carducci, and a variety of figures and issues in modern and contemporary Italian literature; he is also editor of a volume of essays on Orwell's *Nineteen Eighty-Four* and its implications for life today. Since 1976 he has been on the faculty of the Ohio State University at Columbus where he teaches contemporary and modern Italian literature and has served as acting associate dean of the College of Humanities and in the Program in Comparative Studies in the Humanities.

Preface

In recent years there has been a resurgence of interest in Gabriele D'Annunzio and his work. Condemned or ignored earlier, first as a literary bully who preferred noisy fustian to clarity of expression, then as a political figure thoroughly compromised by his associations with Fascism, finally as an aggressive and shameless sexist, D'Annunzio has now returned to historical prominence as the dominant influence that he was in turn-of-the-century Italy. D'Annunzio's nonmimetic poetics, indifference to truthful replication but faith in writing as a means of self-definition, and belief in the equivalence of sexual, political, and artistic desire are only a few aspects of his thinking that tie his work to contemporary critical debate. Fifty years after his death, moreover, it has become clear that it is unnecessary to like D'Annunzio in order to take an interest in who he was and what he stood for. Prolific, successful, and once much admired both in and outside Italy, D'Annunzio can be ignored only at the risk of impoverishing our understanding of crucial social, psychic, and literary realities over nearly fifty years of modern Italian and European history.

Although there have been several biographies of D'Annunzio in English and a good deal of passing reference to him in specialized work as well, the study that follows is the first full-length English-language consideration of all of this writer's major literary works. In a guide of this sort it has not been possible to discuss every one of D'Annunzio's collected and uncollected compositions as they appear in the more than fifty volumes of his writings, or to treat the works that are discussed with the thoroughness appropriate to more specialized investigations. The major literary texts, however, have all been at least touched on here in an account that is meant to be critical as well as informative.

D'Annunzio's literary activity falls with only some overlap into a series of ten-year, largely self-contained periods, each of which was devoted to a different literary genre. The chapters that follow, consequently, have been arranged by both genre and decade, treating in turn the poetry and stories of the 1880s, the society writing, poetry, and novels of the 1890s, then, in the new century, the plays, the later poetry, and finally the memorialistic writing toward the end of the poet's life. Since D'Annunzio's life is reflected so directly in his writing,

GABRIELE D'ANNUNZIO

I have preferred not to summarize it in the book's first chapter, choosing instead to discuss his lived life along with his written one—specular images so similar in his case that it is often difficult to tell which is the event and which the reflection. Readers interested in a summary of D'Annunzio's life and accomplishments (including his amorous liaisons) may consult one of the numerous extant biographies, as well as the Chronology that follows this preface.

The recent revival of D'Annunzio studies in Europe and America has been fostered by two outstanding scholars: Emilio Mariano in Italy and Paolo Valesio in the United States. Along with many others—Guy Tosi in France; Ezio Raimondi, Paolo Alatri, Pietro Gibellini, and Federico Roncoroni in Italy; plus a younger generation (many of whom have been Valesio's students) in this country—these two critics have shaped the way D'Annunzio is thought about today and it is a pleasure for me to be able to thank them for their support of this project. Thanks also are due to Elena Ledda and the staff of the D'Annunzio museum, library, and archives of Il Vittoriale degli Italiani at Gardone where I spent some extremely happy days in the summer of 1986. I am grateful as well to Dean Micheal Riley and the College of Humanities of the Ohio State University for the travel grant that helped make that trip possible. Thanks too to Davies Menefee and Eva Godwin of the Ohio State University library system who provided important research support. I would also like to thank Don Larson for his help with the final editing of the manuscript, and Anthony Oldcorn, Twayne's field editor for Italian literature, for inviting me to contribute to this series in the first place.

Charles Klopp

The Ohio State University

Acknowledgments

Permission to quote and translate from *Tutte le opere di Gabriele D'Annunzio* has been granted from the Fondazione Il Vittoriale degli Italiani through the kind offices of Professor Pietro Gibellini. The frontispiece photograph is from the collection in the Foundation's Gabinetto Fotografico.

Chronology

1863 Gabriele D'Annunzio born 12 March in Pescara (Abruzzi).

1874 Student at the Reale Collegio Cicognini in Prato.

1879 *Primo vere* published in Chieti.

1880 *In memoriam.*

1881 Graduated from the Cicognini; newspaper work in Rome; relationship with Elda Zucconi ("Lalla").

1882 *Canto novo* and *Terra vergine* published by Sommaruga.

1883 End of relationship with Elda Zucconi; marriage to Maria Hardouin di Gallese; birth of son Mario.

1884 · *Intermezzo di rime; Terra vergine; Il libro delle vergini;* brief relationship with Olga Ossani.

1886 *Isaotta Guttadàuro ed altre poesie; San Pantaleone;* birth of son Gabriellino.

1887 Relationship with Barbara Leoni ("Barbarella"); birth of son Veniero.

1889 *Il piacere;* military service.

1890 *L'Isottèo–La Chimera;* end of military service and separation from Maria Hardouin; relationship with Maria Gravina.

1892 *Giovanni Episcopo; L'Innocente; Elegie romane;* end of relationship with Barbara Leoni.

1893 *Odi navali/Poema paradisiaco;* birth of daughter Renata; death of D'Annunzio's father.

1894 *Trionfo della morte.*

1895 *Le vergini delle rocce;* trip to Greece with Scarfoglio; beginning of relationship with Eleonora Duse ("Ermione").

1896 End of relationship with Maria Gravina.

1897 Election to Parliament on right-wing ticket; *Sogno d'un mattino di primavera.*

1898 *La città morta; Sogno d'un tramonto d'autunno;* move to "Capponcina" at Settignano, near Florence; trip with Duse to Egypt and Greece.

1899 *La Gioconda; La gloria.*

1900 *Il fuoco.*

1902 *Le novelle della Pescara; Francesca da Rimini.*

1903 *Maia (Laus vitae);* relationship with Alessandra di Rudinì ("Nike").

1904 *Elettra/Alcyone; La figlia di Iorio;* end of relationship with Eleonora Duse.

1905 *La fiaccola sotto il moggio.*

1906 *Più che l'amore.*

1907 Relationship with Giuseppina Mancini ("Amaranta"); end of relationship with Alessandra di Rudinì.

1908 *La nave; Solus ad solam* (published 1939); end of relationship with Giuseppina Mancini; relationship with Natalia de Goloubeff ("Donatella").

1909 *Fedra.*

1910 *Forse che sì forse che no;* severe difficulties with creditors and beginning of residence in France.

1911 *Le Martyre de Saint Sébastien;* performance in Paris with music by Debussy, sets by Bakst, and Ida Rubinstein in the title role.

1912 *Merope; Contemplazione della morte.*

1913 *La Pisanelle ou la mort parfumée.*

1914 *Il ferro.*

1915 Return to Italy; end of relationship with Natalia de Goloubeff; entrance of Italy into World War I; D'Annunzio at the front.

1916 *La Leda senza cigno;* relationship with Olga Levi ("Venturina"); military flights over enemy lines and loss of right eye.

1917 Torpedo boat excursion into Buccari harbor; death of D'Annunzio's mother.

1918 Flight over Vienna and leaflet bombardment.

1919 End of relationship with Olga Levi; forceful occupation of Fiume where D'Annunzio is declared "Comandante"; relationship with Luisa Baccara.

1921   End of Fiume occupation and move to Lake Garda; *Notturno*.

1922   "March on Rome" and beginning of Fascist Era.

1923   Il Vittoriale degli Italiani made national monument.

1924   First volume of *Le faville del maglio;* named Prince of Montenevoso.

1927   First volume of "Edizione Nazionale" of complete works.

1928   Second volume of *Le faville del maglio*.

1935   *Libro segreto*.

1936   Edizione Nazionale completed (49 vols.).

1938   1 March, death from a cerebral hemorrhage.

Chapter One

The Red Flower of Youth: Poetry and Prose of the 1880s

The D'Annunzio Enigma

In a passage in his *Italian Hours* comparing the difficulty of expressing the beauty he sees and feels around him in Capri to a metaphorical tax he must pay for "the luxury of loving Italy," Henry James has this to say about D'Annunzio: "For a certain art of asking of Italy all she can give," he writes, "you must doubtless either be a rare *raffiné* or a rare genius, a sophisticated Norseman or just a Gabriele D'Annunzio."[1] Although it is evident that James had reservations about some of his Italian counterpart's accomplishments, both from the adverb and the maliciously indefinite article in the phrase, "just a Gabriele D'Annunzio," in this passage the American writer not only admits that D'Annunzio is a rare genius but seems a bit envious of his ability to elicit "all she can give" from the land that both authors loved, if in different ways.[2]

However serious James may have been in this passage, and whatever the value of this image of D'Annunzio as successful solicitor of Italy's favors, this comment in the *Italian Hours* makes clear with what seriousness—and suspicion—D'Annunzio was viewed by the international literary establishment of the day. A similar admiration, and similar reservations, have been part of critical attitudes to this writer ever since.

Critical Fortunes and Misfortunes

Almost everyone agrees that for virtuoso technique, there have not been many Italian writers—at least not since the seventeenth-century Neapolitan poet Giambattista Marino—able to match D'Annunzio as a master of literary razzle-dazzle. At the same time, although not many figures in the history of Italian literature enjoyed a more enthusiastic reception during their lifetimes, fewer still have later fallen to comparable depths of critical silence and supposed "unreadability."

Nonetheless, D'Annunzio, like sin or taxes—or the historical fact of Italian Fascism—will not go away. Like him or not, D'Annunzio was the dominant influence on Italian literature in the first part of this century and his example still looms in much of Italy's current prose, poetry, and oratorical style. But D'Annunzio was more than a writer. He was a public figure who impressed himself on the collective consciousness of Western Europe not only because of the excitement generated by his poetry, novels, plays, and other writings, or because of his ability to impose himself on the public eye through theatrical displays of prowess as man of action and spectacular lover, but also because he was able to articulate a political and social ideology congenial to the European middle classes at the beginning of the industrial era in Italy.

Not only did D'Annunzio's narratives spawn a host of popular novels in which his more lurid explorations of erotic behavior were aped and inflated; not only did his poetry cause by reaction the deliberately understated writing of the "crepusculars" and such minimalist poets as Giuseppe Ungaretti; twentieth-century social life was also lastingly affected by his example. Toward the end of the twentieth century D'Annunzio's presence could be felt in such different areas of Italian life as the dialogue heard at the cinema, the style employed in personal letters, popular and scholarly writing—even the rhetoric of seduction.

Given his overwhelming early commercial success and the later flow of many of the expressive modalities he invented into the murky waters of Fascist rhetoric, it is not surprising that new generations of intellectuals from the Fascist and post-Fascist eras should view D'Annunzio and his works with diffidence or hostility. Beginning with the consolidation of the Fascist regime in the late 1920s and continuing to the years immediately following World War II, in his later years D'Annunzio came to be viewed first as a grotesque parody of his earlier self and willing receptacle for current establishment values, then as a distasteful reminder of a hateful and repudiated regime.

It is only now, almost fifty years after his death and nearly as many since the demise of the political system with which he was sometimes unfairly identified, that a measured appraisal of this writer's work has begun to be possible. In his last years D'Annunzio was consigned by Mussolini to the gilded cage of his Garda villa, Il Vittoriale degli Italiani, where he lived out his days as an ideological mummy sealed off from everyday life. Until recently, much of the criticism written about him has similarly embalmed his writings in the malodorous fluids of the political views they seem to adopt. Only in the last decades has the critical silence surrounding D'Annunzio begun to be breached, as his texts are reexamined in the light of current critical concerns.[3]

Pescara

Gabriele D'Annunzio was born 12 March 1863, in the Adriatic seacoast town of Pescara in the Abruzzi region of southeastern Italy. He was the son of *galantuomini*, the newly emergent southern middle class of the recently united Kingdom of Italy. Gabriele's father had been born Francesco Paolo Rapagnetta, but took the name D'Annunzio after he was adopted by his uncle, the childless merchant and shipowner Antonio D'Annunzio. In addition to a slightly more elegant last name, Francesco Paolo Rapagnetta inherited a modest fortune from Antonio D'Annunzio, and his own five children—in order of birth, Anna, Elvira, Gabriele, Ernestina, and Antonio—grew up in circumstances that were comfortably middle-class. A man of strong physical appetites, Francesco Paolo was eventually to squander both his own and his children's shares of the family fortune in his pursuit of such opportunities for dissipation as Pescara offered. He was never treated with much affection in his son's writings where he appears, for example, as the model for Giorgio Aurispa's feckless and philandering father in the *Trionfo della morte* *(Triumph of Death)* of 1894. In addition to having a keen eye for women, however, Francesco Paolo was sufficiently perspicacious to be aware of the intellectual gifts his firstborn son possessed and of the threat to his intellectual development posed by life in culturally restricted Pescara. Accordingly, and in a move that was to prove decisive for the intellectual and artistic growth of the future writer, in 1874 he packed off the precocious eleven-year-old to the academically rigorous and socially prestigious Cicognini boarding school at Prato, near Florence, in many ways still the cultural capital of United Italy. It was as a transplanted southerner at this Tuscan school that Gabriele began his education in the classical and Italian literary traditions that were to serve him so well throughout his life as a writer.

D'Annunzio's memories of his early years in Pescara are not always idyllic, at least not in the reminiscences that he published as an old and famous man thinking back about his childhood. They include descriptions of such sharply traumatic experiences as the death of a favorite horse while D'Annunzio and his sisters watch in terror, and the destruction by the family steward of the swallow nests accumulated beneath the eaves of the D'Annunzio house. A more heroic childhood memory concerns D'Annunzio's stabbing himself with a jackknife while trying to open a mollusk given him by a fisherman. Frightened at the wound and angered at his ineptness, the boy managed to open the shell anyway and devour the creature inside before returning home, light-headed and dripping blood, but aware as never before of the mysterious predestination guiding his life.

Prato

In addition to studying Latin and Greek, at the Cicognini the young D'Annunzio quickly assumed the social and cultural postures that were to be his for the rest of his life. An excellent student who was almost always first in his class, he made the most of his superior native intelligence and extraordinary verbal abilities by diligent application to his studies, often laboring through the night at his lessons, a work habit that he was to maintain throughout his career. At the Cicognini, D'Annunzio exchanged his southern accent and regional speech patterns for the Tuscan inflections and vocabulary that reigned in the school, from this time forward adopting a purist linguistic posture that rivaled that of the most pedantic among his teachers. Although he studied Italian literature, history, geography, sciences, music, and mathematics, as well as Latin and Greek at the Cicognini, it was in this latter field especially that he excelled. By the time he completed his schooling, he had managed to assimilate the stylistic traits and thematic preoccupations of the writers of antiquity into his own literary and linguistic repertory. Although some commentators have had reservations about the depth of D'Annunzio's cultural and literary knowledge—especially his abilities with abstract thought and philosophical notions—there seems little doubt that in the field of literature, even as a schoolboy D'Annunzio was a force to be reckoned with.

Primo vere

D'Annunzio was only sixteen and still a student when in 1879 he published his first volume of verse, *Primo vere* (First spring). A second edition was issued the following year, just after someone—almost certainly the poet himself—had spread the rumor of the tragically premature (but commercially opportune) death of its author. The thirty brief lyrics that make up the first *Primo vere* are modeled ostentatiously on the

Odi barbare of Giosue Carducci (1835–1907). In the three volumes of his "Barbarous Odes," the first of which was published in 1877, Carducci, Italy's leading poet of the time (and in 1906 the winner of the Nobel Prize for literature), had broken with the Italian metrical tradition of syllabic and stress-organized verse by turning for his models to the quantitative meters of Greek and Latin antiquity. In following Carducci's lead for the metrical shape of the poems in his first volume of poetry, D'Annunzio was attempting to insert himself into the process of renovation of Italian poetry and culture begun by the older poet and to cash in on the popularity of the innovative poetic forms associated with him. At one point D'Annunzio even considered calling his collection *Odi arcibarbarissime* (Extra-super-barbarous odes), though it is not entirely clear whether such a title would have suggested that his own work fell short of or surpassed that of his predecessor.

The 1880 second and revised edition of *Primo vere*, characterized by its adolescent author as having been "corrected with pen and fire," is different in several ways from the first. The introductory poem to Carducci and the "Ora satanica" (Satanic hour), a transparent imitation of the older poet's notorious "A Satana" (To Satan) have disappeared, along with about half of the texts in the original collection. The new *Primo vere* is expanded too, consisting now of fifty-three poems in "barbarous" and traditional meters plus a concluding group of translations from the Greek and Latin. Altogether, the new edition makes a strong case that even in the short space of a year D'Annunzio has grown both as a writer and as an editor of his own writing. Although echoes of various Italian neoclassical poets can be heard behind many of the lines here, it is still Carducci who dominates D'Annunzio's poetic imagination. This is evident not only in the language employed and subjects treated, but even in such details as D'Annunzio's choice of Lilia (compare Carducci's "Lidia") for the name of the woman praised in the volume.

Noteworthy among the evocations of Florentine and Abruzzi landscapes and the poetic gallantries to a variety of different women that make up much of this volume are two series of poems at its conclusion: the "Studii a guazzo" (Studies in gouache) and "Idilli selvaggi" (Savage idylls). The first are genre studies of peasant life in terms suggestive of the "veristic" style of naturalistic prose made famous by Giovanni Verga in these same years—a style that D'Annunzio himself will employ in his short fiction of the 1880s. In the seven "pythiambic" odes of the "Idilli selvaggi" a summer love affair plays itself out against the

passing of the months from June to December, an organizational ploy
that will be famously and magisterially developed much later in D'Annunzio's *Alcyone* of 1904. For all of his schoolboyish tendencies in this
volume, this is a surprisingly able performance for so young a writer.
Significant too are the differences between this work and the Carduccian
model, among them the way the sharp plasticity of the older author's
poetry gives way to a resolution of poetic tensions in music, a strategy
that will become a hallmark of much of D'Annunzio's later verse as
well. For the moment, these are poems that brim with youthful
exuberance and show the young poet's eagerness to experiment with
whatever seems most vital in the literary and cultural traditions that
have so far become accessible to him.

In Memoriam

D'Annunzio's second book of verse was much less successful than
his first one and today is all but forgotten. The twenty somewhat
sentimental sonnets on the death of his grandmother collected in 1880
as *In Memoriam* do fall short of the expectations set by the Abruzzese
wunderkind with *Primo vere*. The young poet himself must have sensed
that the new book represented a mistaken direction and in *Canto novo*
(New song) of 1882, his second significant collection, he returned to
the Carduccian high road that he had marched along so vigorously in
Primo vere. Although traditional rhymed sonnets are included in this
book too, most of the new texts are once again in the unrhymed
"barbarous" meters reintroduced by Carducci.

Sommaruga

In the brief period between the second edition of *Primo vere* in 1880
and the first edition of *Canto novo* in 1882 D'Annunzio had not only
tasted the heady brew of success, but had matured significantly as a
writer. After all, he was now no longer a stripling poet of sixteen but
a seasoned nineteen-year-old author. As such, he did not hesitate to
submit his newest batch of poems, together with the prose sketches he
had been writing in this same period, to the prestigious Bolognese
publishing house of Zanichelli—the publisher of Carducci's *Odi barbare,*
among other serious and successful works. Zanichelli, however, decided
not to include either one of D'Annunzio's proposed collections in its
list. Undaunted, the young author turned instead to the Roman publisher

Angelo Sommaruga.[4] Sommaruga was the promotional intelligence behind the flamboyant *Cronaca bizantina* (Byzantine chronicle), a periodical to which D'Annunzio was later to contribute, and an exponent of the so-called American style of publishing—that is, the treatment of printed matter as objects of commerce first and contributions to literary culture only secondarily. Sommaruga, whose innovative publishing practices were to lead to a number of duels and an eventually ruinous lawsuit, was a central figure in the raffish maelstrom of Roman journalism into which D'Annunzio was impatient to plunge. Sensing, perhaps, that the young Abruzzese represented what was most commercially viable in the production of the newest generation of writers, he agreed to publish both the lyrics of *Canto novo* and the stories of *Terra vergine.*

Canto novo

As its title proclaims, *Canto novo* is meant to be a "new song" lifted by a brasher and more vigorous voice than Carducci's stentorian and authoritative but by now overly sedate baritone. Although the precedent set by the *Odi barbare* is still evident, especially metrically, in much of the work in this volume, its language and subject matter show that D'Annunzio is now clearly his own person. Nowhere is this more evident than in the attitude taken in these lyrics toward ancient Greece and Rome. In the exuberant pantheism of the *Canto novo,* the classical world is no longer, as it was for Carducci, an incentive to civic virtue and moral regeneration in a reborn "Third Italy" worthy of taking its rightful place alongside those of the Caesars and the Renaissance Popes. For D'Annunzio in this book, classical precedent has no other function than to serve as an invitation to sensual pleasure. In it the traditional paeans to life, love, and nature in a world where youth is fleeting and death comes all too soon, have slipped the restraints that Carducci and other classicizing poets had imposed on them, as the austere Greek temple of neoclassical tradition is made to blink with the gaudy neon of a new hedonism indifferent to conventional morality.

Much of *Canto novo* was written in response to a personal experience of great importance for D'Annunzio: his love for Elda Zucconi, the first real love of his life. A spirited girl about his own age and the daughter of one of D'Annunzio's professors at the Cicognini, Elda was the "E.D." of the book's dedication as well as the "Strana bimba da gli occhioni erranti, / misteriosi e fondi come il mare" (Strange girl with large wandering eyes / deep and mysterious as the sea) of its dedicatory sonnet. Although all references to her disappeared from the revised, 1896 edition of the collection, at least in the first version of *Canto novo* it is the magic of Elda as "Lalla" that has bewitched the poet's erotic and artistic imagination.

The sixty-three lyrics of the 1882 *Canto novo* are arranged into five sections prefaced by a sonnet to Elda and a "Preludio" (Prelude). The elegiac couplets of the latter describe a young man swimming in the Pescara river in a natural environment that pulses with powerful sensual stimulation: the visual beauty of the Abruzzi riverscape, the feel of sun and water upon the swimmer's body, the smells of the wildflowers and musk from the *cerambici* beetles along its banks, the sounds of the rustling stream and birds along its shores. In his description of these visual, tactile, olfactory, and auditory stimuli and their effect upon his central character D'Annunzio deliberately blurs the usual biological categories in metaphors in which plants are compared to animals as well as to other plants, and the protagonist of the poem merges psychologically and spiritually into the botanical and zoological world in which he is physically immersed.

In the poems that follow this "Preludio" the theme of metamorphosis will be further developed in an exaltation of the unity of all living things, whether human, animal, or vegetable. This affirmation of natural life takes place in a precisely described natural setting: the unspoiled Abruzzi of the poet's childhood, a land drenched by the sun and washed by the sea ("Thàlatta! Thàlatta!" the poet exclaims excitedly—and in Greek—toward the end of the next poem). When Lalla arrives in this landscape to play "panther" or "antilope" to his "jaguar," the poet calls on her to spur his poetic activity to even greater heights:

> Per te germogli l'ecloga a gli ozii
> de 'l pomeriggio, tra la salsedine
> de' venti marini, fra i trilli,
> in un chiosco d'aranci in fiore;
>   per te le frutta auree occhieggino
> tra 'l verde cupo, ne l'Adriatico
> lontano si perda uno sciame
> di vele rosse, tacciano i lidi,
>   Lalla, ed io vegga su le tue pallide
> gote improvviso aprire i calici
> il roseo fior del disio,
> ne gli occhi fulvi ridere il sole,
>   schiuderti io vegga la bocca simile

a melagrana . . . ch'io senta fremerti
la bocca odorosa di arancia,
fresca, vermiglia, ne 'l bacio mio.
(2.7)[5]

[Let my eclogue germinate for you in the afternoon's leisure, in the salt spray of the ocean breezes and of the birdsongs, in the flowering orange trees' cloister; let the golden fruit wink for you in the midst of the green shadow, while a swarm of red sails disappears on the distant Adriatic. Let the shores fall silent, Lalla, while I see the pink flower of desire suddenly open its chalices on your pale cheeks and the sun smile yellow in your eyes, and your mouth open like a pomegranate . . . and I feel your mouth fragrant as an orange tremble cool and vermilion beneath my kiss!][6]

This too is a poem of sharp and powerful physical sensations. In the first stanza alone these include the feel of the salty sea breeze, the sound of the birds, and the pungent smell and sight of the orange blossoms. Like many other texts throughout this volume, the poem is filled with vivid chromatic effects: the gold fruit, green shade, and red sails of the Adriatic seascape, Lalla's cheeks which are first pale but then flush pink with desire as the sun shines yellow in her eyes, and finally the cool vermilion of her trembling, fragrant mouth beneath the poet's kiss. Once again natural life is imbued with human characteristics as the fruit "winks," the shores "fall silent," and the sun "laughs." Similarly, human life blends with animal and vegetable existence as "eclogues germinate," boats disappear like bees in a "swarm" of sails, desire is a "pink flower [that] opens its chalices," and Lalla's mouth is as red as a pomegranate, fragrant and cool as an orange. Poetry too participates in the pantheistic fervor as D'Annunzio calls to his eclogue itself to "germinate" in response to his lady's imagined arrival, an exhortation that bears literal fruit in the pomegranate and orange of the text's conclusion.

It should also be noticed that the poet's joy at being with Lalla in this powerfully sensual setting is matched by his exultation at writing the poem that celebrates this moment, an activity that would seem to have little to do with midnight oil or the *labor limae* (file's labor) of classical tradition. Elsewhere in this section D'Annunzio had said good-bye to the "genteel army" of books that used to keep him ghostly company during his chilly nights of study. Like the painters in both Italy and France during this same period, who abandoned what had come to seem the fusty air of the studio in favor of outdoor settings for their painting, D'Annunzio wanted his poems in this volume to be not academic exercises, but new songs lifted *en plein air* beneath the brilliant Abruzzi sunlight.

In this volume sensuality is more than the supreme value of natural life; it is also the principal means that humans have of apprehending the world. In a later poem in the same volume D'Annunzio describes a sexual assault on a peasant girl who, already "violated by the sun," is chased and seized by an unnamed lover until they couple in the underbrush "like two snakes in heat." As his hero grapples with his peasant prey like an ancient gladiator struggling with a panther, the site of their encounter is transformed into a Roman amphitheater as the poet calls on the surrounding trees, hills, and sea to applaud the successful combat: "Plaudite plaudite plaudite, / come un popolo a 'l circo, piante, colline, mare!" (1.8.21–22)

A passage like this is notable not only for what it reveals about D'Annunzio's sexual predilections, need for approval, and striking lack of self-irony, but also for its presentation of sensuality as a means to master an otherwise recalcitrant universe, a world which here not only submits to this domination but literally applauds the effort. Although in his later work D'Annunzio will move away from an examination of the phenomenology of nature developed in these early lyrics to a more pronounced antinaturalism of the sort usually associated with the decadent movement, he will remain firm in his belief that violently sensual experience can serve as an epistemological lever to pry open the mysteries of material reality.

Despite the sensual abandon of most of the lyrics in this collection, certain poems, especially in book 3, sound a quite different note of social, even socialist protest. In a letter to Elda's father about the book D'Annunzio describes its "discharges of ferocious socialism" that foreshadow a future "great social poem."[7] The inclusion of rather bleak poems on social themes in this otherwise joyous volume may be explained in part by its author's awareness of the success of the naturalist movement in Italy, especially the stories and sketches of his contemporary, Giovanni Verga (1840–1922). While at the Cicognini, D'Annunzio had also read *The Origin of Species,* and the weight of Darwin and positivism can also be felt throughout *Canto novo.* By the new edition of 1896, however, he recognized that such texts were discordant notes in his otherwise ecstatic "new song," and omitted them from the definitive version.

Terra vergine

D'Annunzio's first narrative work, the nine (later eleven) naturalistic stories of *Terra vergine* (Virgin land), was brought out by Sommaruga in the same month of 1882 as *Canto novo*. Brief tales of peasants, fishermen, beggars, and other social outcasts, these stories are set in the same pristine and energetic Abruzzi of *Canto novo* and share that volume's penchant for bright colors and a frequent insistence on the similarities between vegetable, animal, and human life, though in a context of a bitter and often brutal struggle for survival that has nothing of the pantheistic joy of the other volume. Where the poet-protagonist of *Canto novo* had glorified in the purity and urgency of the animal passions, in *Terra vergine* the passions—especially lust and jealousy— lead quickly to tragedy and death. This is partly because these powerful emotions are not just interludes for such city folk on vacation as the poet and his Lalla, but represent a painful eruption in the everyday working lives of the actual inhabitants of the region, the same rural proletariat described in despairing terms in book 3 of *Canto novo*. Although *Terra vergine* too provides its readers with an opportunity for vicarious delight in raw, animal existence, this pleasure cannot help but be tempered by dismay at the plight of the easily stirred, mostly inarticulate, and emotionally defenseless people who figure in its pages.

When compared to the positions taken by other writers, ethnographers, and folklorists during this time of interest and concern for peasant life and "la questione sociale," D'Annunzio's attitude toward his subjects may be somewhat short on fellow feeling and human sympathy. The literary exploration of peasant life that he began with *Terra vergine* and was to continue in such later works as the *Trionfo della morte* and *La figlia di Iorio,* was for D'Annunzio a foray into an aspect of existence with which—try as he might—he was never able to identify and finally found repellent. D'Annunzio's peasants, far from attaining the epic dignity that is the achievement of the most positive among Verga's characters, are so dehumanized by poverty and ignorance as to appear more like exhibits of savagery brought for display from some remote place on the globe than dignified epigones of a lost heroic age.

This is partly because Verga is careful to insert his characters into a precisely defined historical context while the rural lumpen proletariat of D'Annunzio's stories seem located at a degree zero of historicity, a point before the advent of historical time or the establishment of civilization. Where Verga's characters are both participants in history and members

of social groups defined by distinct rules passed down from generation
to generation (rules encapsulated, for example, in the many proverbs
that run through his novel *I Malavoglia* [*The House by the Medlar
Tree*] of 1882), D'Annunzio's are as indifferent to such social strictures on their thoughts or conduct as the animals with whom they
live in tight but easy symbiosis and with whom they are frequently
merged in the many metaphors comparing humans and beasts in these
narratives.

   Thus, in the book's title story the swineherd Tulespre captures and
copulates with the goatherd Flora in a gesture authorized by the powerful
stimulation his simple organism has received from the ethically indifferent
natural world around him, the only frame of reference that matters to
Tulespre, and the only one in which his behavior can be understood
or judged. In this book D'Annunzio's characters respond to elemental
emotions of love and hate in an environment where biological and
zoological forces dominate and social or ethical considerations are irrel-
evant. When, in the next story, Dalfino kills the customs officer who
is his rival for Zarra's love, he does not go to trial and then to jail
like the 'Ntoni who is guilty of the same crime in *I Malavoglia*.
Dalfino, instead, decides his own fate by leaping into the sea and
swimming out to drown. In so doing, he has chosen a mode of
punishment that has nothing to do with such historical and human
constructions as that of the state and its system of legal justice, but is
defined instead only by his own biological condition as a land-dwelling
animal unable to survive for long in the sea. In this volume D'Annunzio
has extended the notion of a Darwinian "struggle for life" from an
evolutionary biological context to a primitive and still uncohesive social
sphere. For this reason, many of the characters in this early book are
outcasts struggling for survival on the periphery of human society: the
mad or mentally retarded like the village idiot in "Cincinnato," Biasce
in "Campane" (Bells), or the hydrocephalic baby of "Lazzaro," the
beggars who die in the snow at the end of "Toto," or the gypsies of
"Ecloga fluviale" (Fluvial eclogue). The cruelty that these and other
characters in this book endure (Toto has had his tongue cut out by
brigands, Biasce hangs himself in a church steeple, Nora in "Bestiame"
[Livestock] copulates with her father-in-law while her husband is dying
of typhoid in the next room) seems the inevitable lot of the weak or
handicapped in a neo-Darwinian struggle for survival in which the
stronger not only prevail but also take a perverse pleasure in doing so.

Il libro delle vergini

The publication in 1884 of *Il libro delle vergini* (The book of the virgins) led to a break between D'Annunzio and Sommaruga, ostensibly because of a dispute over the volume's cover. Its four stories all have middle-class settings and center on characters who are far more wracked by inhibitions than the straightforward peasants of *Terra vergine*. In the opening tale of "Le vergini" (The virgins) the spinster Giuliana recovers from a nearly fatal typhoid attack to embrace the life of nature and the body with such long-repressed enthusiasm that she ends up exchanging her virginity for an early death from an awkward abortion attempt. In "Favola sentimentale" (Sentimental fable) Cesare's sexual timidity makes him an easy and willing prey for his more experienced aunt, and in "Nell'assenza di Lanciotto" (In Lanciotto's absence) Francesca and her brother-in-law Gustavo are overcome by an incestuous passion to which Francesca's dying mother is an ashamed and reluctant witness. By the time he wrote "Nell'assenza di Lanciotto" D'Annunzio had become familiar with the work of such contemporary French authors as Emile Zola and Guy de Maupassant. Partly due to their influence, in *Il libro delle vergini* he has abandoned the reluctance to articulate a character's unspoken thoughts that was so typical of the "objective" Verga and his school. The influence of Zola and the French naturalists can also be seen in the clinical detail of the descriptions of such matters as the effects of typhoid fever on the human organism (described at length in "Le vergini") or the account of Giuliana's death from abdominal bleeding after the botched abortion attempt.

In these early stories there are other suggestions of important themes and figures of the later fiction. Francesca, for example, of "Nell'assenza di Lanciotto," is a sophisticated and intellectually complex woman quite unlike the brutal females of *Terra vergine,* and as such a forerunner of the beautiful, knowing, and often cynical women of D'Annunzio's later novels. For her part, the defenseless Giuliana, though almost totally innocent of the ways of the world or of men, prefigures the many other sexually liberated women in D'Annunzio's fiction who are punished for their emancipation by illnesses and disfunctions of their reproductive systems.

San Pantaleone/Le novelle della Pescara

In 1886 D'Annunzio brought out a third major collection of short stories, this time with the Florentine publisher, Barbèra. Called *San*

Pantaleone in its first edition, it was republished by Treves in a revised and augmented version in 1902 as *Le novelle della Pescara* (The Pescara stories) and eventually translated into English as *Tales of My Native Town* (New York, 1920). All the compositions of this volume are set in the Abruzzi, and the narrative focus is once again on the power of passion to transform those it touches for good or for ill, though usually for the latter. In "La vergine Anna" (The virgin Anna), a story that seems to have Gustave Flaubert's "Un coeur simple" somewhere behind it, another of D'Annunzio's disappointed spinsters is given a new identity by the simple-minded zealots of the convent where she works who mistake the senility, which has addled her perceptions, softened her brain, and ruined her health, for a special sign from God, and celebrate what becomes her almost vegetablelike condition as saintliness. Unlike Giuliana of "Le vergini" (whose story is reprinted at the beginning of this collection as "La vergine Orsola"), the virgin Anna has been thrust into a new and different life not by the power of eroticism desperately counterposed to death, but by the force of misplaced and ignorant religious zeal.

Other stories in this collection also deal with folk religion and popular superstition. In "Gli idolatri" (The idolators) two towns engage in mortal combat over candles stolen by inhabitants of one town from a church in the other. At its conclusion a kind of rough justice has been reestablished, but it is clear that this is an equilibrium that has nothing to do with notions of Christian forgiveness. In "L'eroe" (The hero) a villager has had his hand crushed beneath a monumental icon of his patron saint which has fallen during a religious procession. Later, in church, the hero of the title kneels at the altar, amputates his now useless hand with a jackknife, and offers it patiently to the saint. In both these stories religious emotion is not put forward as equivalent to sexual desire the way it sometimes is in D'Annunzio, but is tied instead to the equally powerful human urge for destruction. In these compositions the savage rites of a cult of blood, revenge, and violence are unmasked as surrogates for the repressed violence and frustrations of peasant adepts.

Many other stories in this collection are concerned with similarly exceptional behavior, even if few characters can manage the mad determination of the "hero." By stripping away the mask of local color from the folkloric phenomena that he describes in these tales, thereby revealing the true nature of these customs as cruelly chthonic rites with little relation to the usual comforts offered by a religion like Christianity, D'Annunzio is assuming a position for himself as narrator beyond the distortions of conventional morality. In his unmasking of these primitive customs he thus attains a kind of heroic status like that of the heroes in his stories who also transcend the usual human norms and social conventions through an act of transgression.

Many of the stories in this collection are concerned with madness, disease, or death, and dwell on the shameful and grotesque aspects of human corporality. The book is full of obese and otherwise deformed people, and the deaths that conclude many of its stories are often described in disgusting detail. Although this is naturalism to be sure, the struggle for life in D'Annunzio's naturalistic conception is not so much a battle for survival in a difficult world as it is a contest for mastery over others and a battle for sadistic satisfaction. It is clear in these early stories that only such exceptional beings as the Duke of Ofena, Dalfino, or the "hero" of "L'eroe" are able to endure the force of the passions that prey on human life without being destroyed by them. Although such individuals are able to transcend some of the limits of their otherwise brutal existences, they are not transfigured by their experiences—through increased consciousness of their condition, for example—but only transformed into higher exponents of the same brutality. From this point of view, at least, these are profoundly reactionary stories.

Chapter Two

The Conquest of Rome: The Dandy and the Decadent

Rome in the 1880s

In 1885 D'Annunzio's friend and fellow southerner, Matilde Serao, published a novel titled *La conquista di Roma* (*The Conquest of Rome,* New York, 1902). Beginning in 1871 when the capital of Italy was moved south from Florence, Rome had begun to attract a stream of ambitious young and not-so-young people eager to conquer this ancient seat of civilization and corruption. Among those aspiring to such a conquest was D'Annunzio. In 1881, by now a graduate of the Cicognini as well as a published author, he enrolled at the University of Rome determined to make his mark on the capital. Although he later declared himself another of the city's victims—the fatal taste for the luxurious and expensive acquired during these years was to lead to the sea of debts in which he floundered for the rest of his life—in this period D'Annunzio did indeed conquer Rome. Not only did he succeed in becoming an important part of the social and literary life of the capital, the period he spent in the city was an extremely successful one for the development of both his prose style and his public image.

During this period D'Annunzio was able to slough what remained of his provincial mannerisms, replacing them with the fashionable poses of an international dandy perfectly at ease in the "high-life" (to use his own English term) of the capital's aristocratic set. In his *Libro di Don Chisciotte* (Don Quixote's book) Edoardo Scarfoglio, another southern friend and later Serao's husband, described how D'Annunzio was transformed while in Rome from an "ingenuous, modest, and polite" young man into a "calculating, vain, and mealy-mouthed" fop. In Scarfoglio's opinion this change took place because the young poet had incautiously ceded to "all of the sad and sterile joys of popularity," especially the flattery of the fancy women he met when the great Roman houses decided to throw open their doors to the charming provincial.[1] During the decade or so that he spent in Rome, D'Annunzio did meet (and did "cede" just as much as he was able) to a number of titled and beautiful Roman women. He even managed, in what was perhaps his greatest succès de scandale ever, to marry one of them—the "Duchessina" or "little duchess" Maria Hardouin di Gallese.

The Society Reporter

These and other skirmishes in D'Annunzio's campaign to conquer Rome were financed by a new kind of literary activity: writing for the popular Roman newspapers, both daily and weekly, that had sprung up like mushrooms in response to the rain of money that had poured onto the city with the transfer of the national government there. The journalistic writing that D'Annunzio began in the 1880s was the beginning of an activity that he would continue at intervals throughout his career. The periodicals to which he submitted this early work had such colorful names as *Fanfulla* (the name of a character in Massimo D'Azeglio's *Ettore Fieramosca*) and *Fanfulla della Domenica* (Sunday Fanfulla), *Capitan Fracassa* (Captain Blusterer), and *Cronaca bizantina* (Byzantine chronicle)—the last of these an allusion to Carducci's complaint that the Rome of united Italy had more in common with Byzantium at its most decadent than with the virtuous and austere capital that the Risorgimento had dreamed of.

D'Annunzio contributed two sorts of writing to these papers: brief fiction with patrician settings and ironic or surprise endings in the French manner, and "cronache mondane" or society reporting. His success as a practitioner of these genres was immediate and considerable; a recent critic who is himself a widely read author of popular Italian fiction has declared that "such an amiably false and ingenious chronicler has never appeared since in the history of journalism."[2] Although he did not include his newspaper writing in his collected works, and his production of this sort has not received the same critical consideration his other work has, D'Annunzio's Roman journalism represents an important step in the development of his abilities as a writer and his view of himself as the greatest of his own literary creations.

In his society journalism the newly Romanized writer is careful to relegate the provincial life of his other stories to an antiworld located at a considerable distance from the artistic and social milieu he is now describing. Geographically, these works all center on the urban capital rather than the provinces; socially, they are set in high society instead of among the downtrodden; and stylistically, they have more in common

with the "decadent" writing now beginning to issue from France than
with the homegrown naturalism of Italian verismo. Despite their function
as badges of his new social status, however, in these stories and sketches
D'Annunzio is not averse to a certain gentle irony, even—and this is
unique in his corpus—a certain self-irony.

The Fiction of the Man of Fashion

In the fictional sketches of this period the new personality that
D'Annunzio has created for himself is clearly delineated. In these accounts
of seductions achieved or narrowly avoided, of jealous husbands and
capricious and beautiful women in Roman interiors whose carefully
described furnishings are meant to demonstrate the author's understanding
of the very latest in fashion, the explosive jealousy, hatred, and desire
of the Abruzzi stories have lost their power to destroy and become
elements in the amusement patterns of the blasé rich.

In a typical article of this sort, "Biancheria intima" (Lingerie), the
narrator catalogues the colors and styles of the underwear favored by
Roman society women in the 1880s, noting how one widow refused
to doff her most intimate weeds even at the insistence of a new lover
whose tastes evidently did not run to black. Other stories in this group
involve equivocal circumstances or mistakes in identity. In "L'avventura
di Don Giovanni" (Don Giovanni's adventure), for example, the title
character succeeds in persuading a lovely woman to accept having been
abandoned by her lover, only to learn that he is in the wrong apartment
and with a different rejected mistress than he had supposed. In "L'ep-
istolica avventura della Marchesa di Malláre" (The "epistolic" adventure
of the Marchesa of Malláre) the heroine falls in love by correspondence
with a man she has never seen and then is tricked into bed by a
brother of this man's fiancée who has passed himself off as the unknown
letter writer. In "Una donna metodica" (A methodical woman) a husband
discovers that his supposedly virtuous wife not only has several lovers,
but also has been keeping score on their performance according to a
point system in which he himself has done very poorly.

Like the "love accountant" of this story, the women who appear in
these tales are as inventive and maliciously intelligent as they are beautiful,
and usually prove more than a match for the men they encounter. The
descriptions of the Roman grandes dames that D'Annunzio included in
his stories and columns are remarkably detailed and precise as well as
flattering. The masterful employment of high-fashion nomenclature in

these journalistic and fictional pieces shows that the ex-pupil from the Cicognini has been able to learn this exotic terminology as quickly and effectively as he did the Greek and Latin and the purist Tuscan that he used to dazzle his teachers and schoolmates in Prato. Expensive clothes, in addition, excited a profoundly voluptuous interest in D'Annunzio that was part of the fascination he felt for costly things of whatever sort—though that these objects were closely associated with the bodies of beautiful Roman women added to their fetishistic power.

Some of the best pages of this society reporting are descriptions in which clothing and the flesh, the elegant and the slightly *fané* (a favorite word from this period), the beautiful and the cruel, are juxtaposed in a heady mixture of contrasting sensations. Describing a ball, for example, D'Annunzio speaks of "that indefinable odor that gives such a strange fascination to the end of a *soirée;* an odor made up of a thousand different elements, clothing and food, perfumes and wines, flowers and female bodies, a smell at once sharp and uncertain, gentle and strong, sensual and spiritual."[3]

In all of this writing D'Annunzio makes great show of using words from different languages and technical lexicons—fashion, horse racing, interior decorating, and the polyglot chatter of the international set. He does this both to establish his credentials as a master of chic terminology and to indulge in some hedonistic linguistic play not unlike the sporting activities of the aristocrats he is describing. Partly for this reason, the prose that D'Annunzio employs in his depictions of this sometimes brittle and artificial world is a much more ductile and knowing instrument than he has ever used before.

In addition to mastering a new kind of writing—and thereby conquering prose if not Rome—in his newspaper work D'Annunzio was also beginning to assemble a new identity. In the naturalistic stories his narrator, while never as impersonal as the canons of verismo demanded, tended to stick to the background. In the society reporting, however, the first-person, clearly autobiographical speaker of the text is not only a strong stylistic presence but also an important narrative component in the story he is telling. During this period D'Annunzio used both his own and a large number of pen names to sign his work, among them "Il Duca Minimo," "Bull Calf," "Vere de Vere," "Lila-Biscuit," "Miching-Mallecho" (also the name of a horse in *Il piacere*), "Happemouche," "Myr," and "Il barone Cicogna." His temporary assumption of these pseudonyms is evidence of a determination to replace his real background with a new, self-fabricated identity—and perhaps of some uncertainty about who he really was. Still, by the end of his stay in Rome, the young author had made significant progress in the construction of his constantly changing but nonetheless distinctly personal style in both writing and living, and was more aware than ever that keeping in the public eye was essential for at least one kind of success as a writer.

Intermezzo di rime

The first book of poetry that D'Annunzio produced during his stay in Rome did seem devised to keep him in the public eye. Provocation for a lawsuit and the occasion for considerable literary-moralistic commotion in the press, *Intermezzo di rime* quickly became another cause célèbre in D'Annunzio's carefully orchestrated career. The book in its original form was published by Sommaruga in July 1883 but editorially dated 1884. A slightly revised edition, also dated 1884, came out the following year. Ten years later, in 1894, an extensively revised version titled simply *Intermezzo* was published in Naples by Bideri.

Intermezzo di rime is the first of several poetry collections D'Annunzio published in the final two decades of the century. It is often considered a kind of chronicle of the young poet's sexual debaucheries during the 1880s, though what most upset D'Annunzio's critics of this book seems to have been his shameless use of intimate details of his sexual conquest of the woman who in July 1883 was to become his wife and six months later—nine after the seduction described in "Peccato di maggio" (May sin)—gave birth to his son, Mario.

In response to the furor over the Sommaruga volume, as well as to the label of "swinish and impudent" that had been applied to him, D'Annunzio reacted with remarkable coolness. Granting that *Intermezzo di rime* was a "bad little book" of poetry, he insisted that the collection was not pornography but the documentation of "an illness, a mental weakness, a momentary decadence" that had overcome him while in Rome. In the revised 1894 *Intermezzo* D'Annunzio went even further, characteristically accentuating some of the volume's more lurid aspects —in the remarkably explicit "Invocazione" (Invocation), for example— while protesting at the same time that much of its content belonged to a period in his life for which he was now sincerely repentant.[4]

Although the content of *Intermezzo di rime* shows a rejection of Carducci in favor of other models, the volume is not unlike Carducci's own 1887 *Rime nuove* (New rhymes) in that the lyrics in it represent an "intermezzo" or "interval" when the poet has turned away from his previous "barbarous" production to conventional rhymes and meters. For D'Annunzio it is now Baudelaire who is a dominant presence. The first sonnet in the volume, for example, is a depiction of the poet's own *fleurs du mal* in the "malign flowers" of verses that rise like "strange plants" from the rotting and maggot-infested carcass of his heart. Faced with this unnatural springtime, the poet is first anxious, then terrified at what his own "weary human plant" is about to bear. For one thing, the "barbarous and powerful youth" that he hymned so stoutly in *Canto novo* has now expired "in the arms of women." Despite this, he cannot resist the beautiful bodies of the opposite sex "twisting / like the spires of a white, agile snake," and on whose "stiffly blossoming breasts" he "falls exhausted at dawn." In thrall to these temptations, the poet now looks back at the first twenty years of his life as nothing more than a forest of "felled trees" (1.3.3–4, 1.4.1–6, 1.8.14).

Although the world-weary pose struck by this still very young and anything but exhausted poet does seem more a product of his reading than of his debauchery, this volume of poetry represents an important step forward for D'Annunzio. No longer the vigorous but sometimes clumsy provincial, he is now able not only to write texts of this studiedly *maudit* sort, but also to produce deft social poems to accompany the gift of a cushion or a fan, experiment with exotic poetic modalities, as well as create some of the first of his brief and elegant rondeaux.

But it is the longer poems—those that drew most of the fire from D'Annunzio's moralistic critics—that are the most interesting in this collection. The seventy-four alexandrines of the "Peccato di maggio," for example, begin with a description of a walk through an enchanted forest with a "Yella" who D'Annunzio's earliest readers had no difficulty recognizing as the poet's future wife. Sensually accosted, first by a vividly colored sunset and then by brilliant moonlight pouring into the fragrant woods where they are strolling, the two young people give in to the temptations assailing them from the natural world, fall to the ground, and make love, she for the first time. In this "descriptive-erotic-autobiographical idyll,"[5] which is also important as a first example of D'Annunzio's use of the *passeggiata* or stroll as a narrative armature for his poetry, love and death are tightly paired as Yella's body stiffens and her eyes "sink half-extinguished in the wave of pleasure," while her partner too turns pale as an icy chill grips his loins. As in *Canto novo*, here too the natural landscape and the human characters inter-

penetrate as the trees of the forest are compared to athletes wrestling
with the embracing ivy and Yella herself is a long-stemmed flower.

The "Peccato di maggio" ends with an image of the poet laboring
in the night on the text that is the record of his experience. D'Annunzio's
own work on this poem seems to have included the consultation of
certain literary authorities on the experience described in it since the
sexually explicit passages of the work, in particular the description of
the seduction itself, are taken almost word for word from sources in
contemporary French literature. Indeed, it has been remarked that—
whatever D'Annunzio's earliest critics might have thought—in this
part of the text the poet is not so much holding a Roman duchess
named Maria Hardouin di Gallese in his arms as he is embracing a
Maupassant heroine.[6]

The other long poem in this volume is "Venere d'acqua dolce"
(Fresh-water Venus). Written in octaves arranged into five narrative
sections, it describes an encounter with a peasant woman whom the
narrator surprises swimming naked in the Pescara. Although at first he
has to force her to submit to his embraces, the poem's narrator quickly
finds himself exhausted by his partner's amorous enthusiasm—D'Annunzio's first depiction of the sexually insatiable woman who will be
so important in his mature work. Like the "Peccato di maggio," "Venere
d'acqua dolce" also ends with an image of the poet transcribing his
experience in verse. The function of life and of love, it seems, is above
all to produce art.

In the somewhat chaotic collection of disparate lyrics that make up
Intermezzo di rime, D'Annunzio's literary models have shifted from the
Odi barbare to poetry in more traditional forms as the poet moves away
from the primitive impressionism of his early writing to the notions of
art currently promulgated by the decadent movement in France. Still
barely twenty years old, D'Annunzio is attempting to deprovincialize
his writing in a way that will satisfy his own needs and appeal to
bourgeois Italian readers eager to appear up to date with modern literary
fashion. Another installment in D'Annunzio's hot-eyed scrutiny of the
erotic component of human conduct, Intermezzo di rime is also an
indication of how willing this young poet was to experiment with the
expressive modalities of the European decadent movement whose languors
and exquisitely wrought forms represent an entirely different tonality
from that of the vigorous and neoclassical Canto novo, with its exaltation
of life and nature. Whatever the relationship this volume might have
had with a crisis, perhaps of an erotic sort, in the poet's life, it certainly

marks his literary recognition that naturalism would no longer do as a modality for the sort of poetry he wished to create.

Isaotta Guttadàuro ed altre poesie

In *Isaotta Guttadàuro ed altre poesie* (Isaotta Guttadàuro and other poems) of 1886 D'Annunzio continued to experiment with poetic forms from outside the contemporary Italian tradition. In this volume he sets himself a virtuoso task: to reproduce the language and situations of Italian Renaissance and Pre-Renaissance poetry and thus create a literary equivalent of the Pre-Raphaelite painting popular at the time. The work in this volume includes ballads, rondeaux, romances, and poems in *nona rima* as well as the more traditional terza rima and sonnet forms. Many of its compositions had already appeared in newspapers and other periodicals before they were collected in a luxury edition with illustrations by such outstanding artists of the day as Vincenzo Cabianca, Alfredo Ricci, and Giulio Aristide Sartorio.

Despite its fancy format, however, the new collection was greeted with some coolness, and soon provoked a parody, *Risaotto al pomidàuro* or "Toma-ato Risa-otto," which led in turn to a duel between D'Annunzio and his old friend Scarfoglio, who had published but not written the spoof. To add to D'Annunzio's difficulties, the book did not sell well in its expensive format. It was partly for this reason that in 1890 he brought out a cheaper and augmented version, *L'Isottèo–La Chimera (1885–1888)* (Isotteo–The chimera [1885–1888]) in which the "altre poesie" of the first collection have been given a section and title of their own. It is also noteworthy that in the new edition the dates of composition figure as part of the title—an indication that D'Annunzio is already beginning that process of editorial historicizing or mythicizing that will be typical of the rest of his career. Despite the editorial reorganization and inclusion of additional poems, *L'Isottèo–La Chimera* is still something of a grab bag of heterogeneous compositions without the coherence of subject and style that will characterize his later collections.

Both versions of the book begin with a sequence of poems featuring the blonde princess, Isaotta or Isottèo—a figure based on the poet's new wife. The "Book of Isaotta/Isottèo" is not autobiographical, however, at least not in the fashion of *Intermezzo di rime.* The contemporary experience that lies behind it is presented in a highly stylized, ahistorical Pre-Renaissance setting that serves to attenuate its autobiographical implications. Just as in the short stories a fabulous and impossibly primitive Abruzzi had served as background for D'Annunzio's tales of lust and passion, these calmer and more refined demonstrations of poetic virtuosity are set against an equally imaginary Italy as distant in time from their readers as the Abruzzi stories were in space. Its representations of aristocratic life and stylized emotion are legitimized through this contact with a famous period in the history of Italian art and society, though mediated by such late nineteenth-century movements as Walter Pater's aesthetic connoisseurship and the Pre-Raphaelite brotherhood. The archaic metrical forms, vocabulary, and modes of speech employed in the volume are intended not so much to recapture a specific historical past as to legitimize current social practices by linking them to a prestigious era in Italian history. Such an exaltation of past glories at a moment when Italy's share of the world's wealth and attention was not particularly large means that these deliberately apolitical lyrics must also be seen as important first stages in the history of D'Annunzio's growing nationalism.

In his poems on "Isaotta Drops-of-Gold" (the family name is an allusion to Maria's blonde hair as well as to the costly metal) D'Annunzio presents a fictitious world of bygone wealth and luxury—a world of expensively furnished palaces, rich clothing and fabrics, beautiful attendants, purebred horses and dogs, abundant flowers, wine, perfume, and jewels—objects that for D'Annunzio evidently represented the most significant accomplishments of Renaissance Italy.

The best-known texts in the Isaotta/Isottèo section of the collection are "Il dolce grappolo" (The sweet cluster) at its beginning, and the concluding "Epode." The first is a short narrative in *nona rima* about a troubadour who succeeds in claiming a kiss from his lady when he finds the grape cluster of the title hanging abandoned in the vineyard after the harvesters' departure. The dramatic situation, the meter, and the vocabulary are all meant to link the action to an earlier Italy, though the teasing erotic game the lady has set her lover, the preoccupation with rare and costly material possessions, and the poet's constant allusions to literary descriptions by Renaissance and Pre-Renaissance Italian masters make clear the poem's intended aggrandizement of that same aristocracy described by the parvenu society journalist. Disclaiming such ulterior and practical motives, however, in the concluding "Epode" to this section D'Annunzio insists in some very famous lines that the poet's motives must be consonant with those artistic and aesthetic values that are the supreme good in human life:

O poeta, divina è la Parola;
ne la pura Bellezza il ciel ripose
ogni nostra letizia; e il Verso è tutto.

[O poet, the Word is divine; / in pure Beauty heaven has placed / all our happiness; and the Line of verse is everything. (4.12–14)]

La Chimera

Although the descriptions of beautiful women and erotic situations that fill many of the lyrics of *La Chimera* are couched in the same carefully nonmodern terminology of the earlier section, the social situations here are those of late nineteenth century rather than Pre-Renaissance Italy. Influenced in many cases not by Italian but by French writers from François Villon to Paul Verlaine, many of the poems in this section belong to what Edoardo Sanguineti has dubbed D'Annunzio's "subpoetry"—a type of writing this twentieth-century poet and critic finds more durable than the "risible and imaginary superpoetry" of D'Annunzio's more ambitious work in this genre.[7] Although there is an important narrative dimension to some of the poems in this section—the tale of Jesus' supposed son Eleabani, for example, with his pronounced sexual predilections and remarkable proclamation that it is the flesh rather than the spirit that is holy—the most successful poetry in this group is the lighter, more musical work that Sanguineti considers *sottopoesia*. In these mostly short lyrics the imagistic repertory is the conventional one of roses, lilies, moonlight, the sea, and beautiful women posed against the palaces, villas, gardens, and fountains of the Roman countryside. What provides these otherwise predictable texts with vivacity is D'Annunzio's remarkable ear, his ability to entrust his message almost entirely to the melody his lines create, as what is signified becomes subsumed by the lushness of the signifier. In the refined musicality of such short lyrics as "Dolcemente muor febbraio" (February sweetly dies) or "Come sorga la luna" (As the moon rises) D'Annunzio not only displays a technical ability that is quite extraordinary for so young a poet, but also comes close to creating that "pure poetry" that aesthetically minded poets have often dreamed of.

Elegie romane

D'Annunzio's next book of poetry was the *Elegie romane* (Roman elegies) of 1892, first published by Zanichelli in Bologna and dedicated to Carducci's friend, Enrico Nencioni. As with previous volumes, much of the work in this collection had already appeared in such magazines as the *Fanfulla della domenica* and the *Nuova Antologia*—a perhaps surprising fact considering their sometimes intimate subject matter, though not if one remembers their author's propensity to broadcast news of his amorous adventures to as wide an audience as possible. All of the poems in this volume are written in elegiac couplets; that is, they follow the quantitative metrics that D'Annunzio had employed in *Primo vere* and *Canto novo,* but not in *Intermezzo di rime* or the Isaotta/Isottèo collection. The twenty-five *Elegie romane* vary in length from the three couplets of "Il pettine" (The comb), a lyric description of a Roman sunset, to the sixty-five distichs of the more narrative "Villa Chigi." Organized into four books of six poems each plus a concluding "congedo," they are a first example in D'Annunzio's corpus of a poetic collection that has been carefully organized into a coherent narrative whole.

By the time he began to write these elegies, Barbara Leoni had taken Maria Hardouin di Gallese's place in D'Annunzio's life and affections, though the story the poems tell is that of her displacement, in turn, by the Sicilian Princess Maria Gravina Cruyllas di Ramacca, who in the early 1890s became D'Annunzio's mistress and in 1893 gave birth to his daughter Renata. In addition to this autobiographical influence, D'Annunzio's *Elegie romane* also had an important literary precedent in Johann Wolfgang von Goethe's *Roemische elegien,* written by the German poet about a century earlier. In their stately vocabulary and classically arranged syntax, replete with inversions and modifiers at considerable distance from the terms they modify, D'Annunzio's elegies look back not only toward Carducci and Goethe, but beyond them to Ovid and other elegiac Roman poets.

Many of the poem's titles are taken from locations in Rome through which the poet is taking a *passeggiata* or stroll. "Il vespro" (Evening), for example, describes his thoughts during a walk along the streets of that city after an afternoon of love. As the poet strolls through the crowded streets, the brilliant colors of the sunset suggest the blood of slaughtered beasts running vermilion against the sky. By the time he arrives in Piazza Barberini these images of gore and violence have been replaced by fantasies of erotic and economic mastery, of "fulgidi amori e lussi mirabili ed ozii profondi; / una più larga forza, una più calda vita" (resplendent loves and marvelous extravagances and profound rest / a hotter and more powerful life). In "Villa d'Este" the "magnificent lady" who accompanies the poet makes the landscape tremble and the fountains gush in submission to her beauty. And at the conclusion of "Elevazione" (Elevation) the poet himself soars into the sky like an eagle—another image of physical potency in which the exceptional being literally rises above the common landscape below.

By book 2, the love hymned in book 1 has begun to disintegrate as the poet is overcome by feelings of sadness, regret, and despair. As the classicizing language of book 1 is displaced by a discourse closer to the patterns of everyday speech, images of pallor, darkness, and death become predominant. In "Sul Lago di Nemi" (On Lake Nemi), for example, the lake is transformed into the river Styx as the lovers sadly note how "everything was dead within us / everything; our love, our pain, our / happiness were nothing but lifeless objects." In "Villa Chigi" the disconsolate couple strolls through a forest where the trees are being felled and the charcoal burners' pyres have been lit. At its end the poet imagines his partner struck down by the woodsman's axe and "lifting her suppliant hands from the red / lake" of her own blood in mute reproach to her companion's coldness. The erotically charged forest of the "Peccato di maggio" has been transformed into a place of physical pain and death. Under these circumstances it is no surprise to find the poet praying in "Il voto" (The vow) for his lady to stop loving him and in this way cease to suffer, while in "In un mattino di primavera" (Spring morning) he imagines her dead on the pillow beside him.

In book 3 these morbid fantasies are partially placated by strolls past such familiar Roman landmarks as St. Peter's, the Tiber, the Pincio park, and Villa Medici. In book 4 the poet has left Rome for Naples in an exile that he compares to Ovid's in Pontus—though the earlier poet did not flee the capital because of bad debts. But even in sunny Naples and with a successor located for his repudiated partner, "Everything seemed solitude / emptiness, sadness, immobile tedium, in the quiet / light, beneath the silent clear distant skies" ("Nella Certosa di San Martino di Napoli" [In St. Martin's Charterhouse in Naples]).

In the often introspective *Elegie romane* D'Annunzio has provided his readers with several variations on the *passeggiata* theme and sketched a number of effective vignettes of famous Roman and Neapolitan landmarks. In these poems of brief joy followed by what seems to be lasting despair, the function of architecture and of history—the whole panoply of the great classical, Renaissance, and baroque monuments of Rome and Naples—is to serve as a mirror for the changing humors of a disaffected lover.

Poema paradisiaco

Although D'Annunzio's next book also organizes occasional poems into a unified narrative, in the *Poema paradisiaco* (Paradisiacal poem—though with a nod to the etymology of "paradise" as "walled park" or "garden") of 1893 he has abandoned the quantitative forms of the *Elegie romane* in what will prove to be a definitive break with this kind of prosody. Once again, many of the poems collected in this volume had already been published in magazines and newspapers, including the daily *Mattino* of Naples, where D'Annunzio was now living with Maria Gravina. In his new work D'Annunzio is not only experimenting with a different mode of expression, but also attempting to give his writing a new moral direction. However, his embrace of goodness, simplicity, and childhood innocence seems more the result of a momentary disgust with contrary values than the outgrowth of a sincere desire for a new kind of existence. D'Annunzio's insistence here on the ethical substance of what he had previously proclaimed the nonmoral nature of artistic activity once again has a literary origin: it was inspired by his reading of the novels of Tolstoy and Dostoyevski, Russian writers of a preceding generation whose books were only at this time beginning to be translated into the Western European languages.

Consistent with its author's newfound morality of abnegation and forbearance in the name of a transcendental though vaguely defined "goodness," the diction of the *Poema paradisiaco* is more restrained and colloquial than ever before in D'Annunzio's writing. In addition, the frequent enjambment, interruptions, ellipses, and parenthetical insertions tend to fragment the poetic discourse it presents, while the assonances and repetition of words and phrases in and among poems give the work an air of dreamy somnambulism. Unlike much of D'Annunzio's other poetry, the lyrics of the *Poema paradisiaco* seem meant to be murmured rather than declaimed. Despite its gentle and unassuming thrust, however, D'Annunzio had planned to give his collection the aggressive title of *Margaritae ante porcos* (that is, pearls [his poetry] before swine [the reading public with which the volume in fact enjoyed great popularity])—a plan that his publisher understandably scotched.

Despite D'Annunzio's antagonistic posture toward his public, the compositions contained in the *Poema paradisiaco* do not make excessive demands on their readers. While the dissolution of metrical and syntactical forms in this poetry may have been suggested to D'Annunzio by the work of his Italian contemporary, Giovanni Pascoli (1855–1912), the principal source for much of its style and many of its images is the work of the French and Belgian symbolists. In this volume the psychological intimacy associated with the symbolists is combined with the moral concern for spiritual regeneration typical of the newly discovered Russian novelists. D'Annunzio's own turn to "goodness," however, originates not so much in ethical conviction as in a longing for less powerful stimulation in an experiential realm that is physical before it is ethical. That the disgust evoked by so many of these poems is a weariness principally of the flesh—and as such only temporary in nature— is made clear by the fact that during the same period that D'Annunzio was at work on these poems he was also writing some of his more salacious additions to the new *Intermezzo*.

There are three main sections in the *Poema paradisiaco*: "Hortus Conclusus" (The closed garden), "Hortus Larvarum" (The garden of ghosts), and "Hortulus Animae" (The little garden of the soul). In a prefatory lyric to the first of these the narrator explicitly repudiates such "horrid" previous writing as his *Intermezzo di rime*, as he substitutes for the firm breasts of that volume the now flacid but once milk-swollen bosom of the weary childhood nurse evoked with kindly affection in the first poem of the new work. Overcome by nostalgia for the innocence and simplicity of an infancy when a woman's body was associated with wholesome sustenance rather than erotic excess, the poet announces in "Il buon messaggio" (Good news) that from now on he will live a simpler life with his mother and sister in his childhood house in the provinces, though in "Nuovo messaggio" (More news), which follows hard after, he suddenly finds that he must break his previous word.

In "Hortus conclusus" the poet is no longer murmuring promises and excuses to his mother and sister, but has assumed his more familiar role as seducer. But he is now a languid, unaggressive swain who thinks of his lady as a closed and inaccessible garden: "Voi, signora, / siete per me come un giardino chiuso" (You, madam / are like an enclosed garden for me). In "La passeggiata" (The stroll) he states discouragedly but matter-of-factly that: "Voi non mi amate e io non vi amo" (I don't love you and you don't love me). In the new and blander landscape of this volume the sky that stretches above these lovers is filled with "vague white apparitions," the ocean "pants softly on the beach," and the poet seems reticent, disheartened, and full of apologies— though it is also clear that both he and his lady are well aware that nothing suits an unkempt garden better than the vigorous husbandry that the narrator seems sure to provide as soon as he can get his strength back.

In "Hortus larvarum" later in the volume, a pair of melancholy lovers wanders through abandoned gardens, past desiccated fountains, unweeded flower beds, and broken statuary—more images from the French symbolists that D'Annunzio was to pass on to the Italian crepuscular poets and to Montale. These are descriptions of missed opportunities, of women who have been loved not too little but not at all, and of "tempi che non sono più"—moments forever past. In "Climene" the title character, clad in a white satin dress and with a broad felt hat shading her weary face and eyes that are "long and transparent as topazes . . . moist with an unshed tear," can only murmur the name "Alceste" as a "dry leaf rustles / entangled on the ground in the hem of her dress." In other poems the passage of time is noted with melancholy resignation as past and future blur into mists of transience, frailty, and death that not even memory is able to dispel.

In "Hortulus animae," the final section, the poet concludes his meditations by vowing again to replace the "cose orrende" or "horrid matters" of previous work with blander and more wholesome visions. Insisting that he is "weary of lying," he intends to go home to his weeping mother on a visit when "Everything will be as it was in the past. / The soul as simple as it used to be, / returning to you, when you call it, as gently / as water that comes to the hollow of your hand" ("Consolazione," [Consolation]). In "O Rus!" (Oh countryside!) his native region is a motherland and provider of "simple gifts" to a poet dreaming of "fresh milk" squeezed from the "swollen udders" of dairy animals whose sole function seems to be to minister to his jaded appetites.

In the epilogue to this volume these regressive postures take on an ideological coloring as a redemptive para-Christian ideology seems to hover blandly like a "new, sublime Dawn" on the poet's horizon. In point of fact, however, the ideological system D'Annunzio is about to embrace is not at all concerned with Christian notions of sacrifice and redemption—except negatively and to reject such gestures as egotistical and self-serving. It was while he was completing the *Poema paradisiaco* that D'Annunzio first came into contact with the philosophy of Friedrich Nietzsche, an encounter that gave all of his writing a new foundation in a philosophical position that had nothing but disdain for conventional notions of "goodness" and "sacrifice."

Although a false turn for him ideologically, the *Poema paradisiaco* is a book of great importance for D'Annunzio the writer. In terms of its influence on succeeding poets, the *Poema paradisiaco* has been second only to *Alcyone,* although such later poets as Gozzano and Montale added a note of irony that was certainly not shared by the "paradisiacal" D'Annunzio.

Odi navali

Contemporary with the *Poema paradisiaco,* and published with it in early editions, are the *Odi navali* (Naval odes). There are eight of these, all on maritime themes and with such titles as "La nave" (The ship), "A una torpediniera nell'Adriatico" (To a torpedo boat in the Adriatic), and "Per la morte dell'Ammiraglio di Saint-Bon" (On the death of Admiral Saint-Bon). Of mostly documentary interest today, the *Odi navali* demonstrate how in the same period of his life D'Annunzio could produce both the intimate and reticent poems of the *Poema paradisiaco* and these quite different declamatory texts that foreshadow the bellicose political writing of his later years.

Intermezzo

During the middle 1890s D'Annunzio also brought out revised editions of two of his earlier collections of poetry: in 1894 *Intermezzo di rime,* now called simply *Intermezzo,* and in 1896 a new version of *Canto novo.* In the revised edition of *Intermezzo di rime* the sentimental poems to the poet's mother have disappeared, as have the brightly colored seascapes. But what really makes the new *Intermezzo* different from *Intermezzo di rime* of ten years earlier is its reorganization of old material and the addition of significant new work. The nine sections of the old collection were labeled "Sonnets of Spring," "Nude Studies," "May Sin," "Old Pastels," "Madrigals," "Fresh-water Venus," "Sleeping Beauty," "To the Poets," and "Purification." In the new edition these have been reduced to a "Prelude" and the five sections, "Sad Animal" (from the Latin tag to the effect that "Every animal is sad after coitus"), "The Adulteresses," "Elegances," "Models," and "Toward the Ancient Joy," a title that reflects the poet's new Nietzschean interests. What in the original edition had been compositions on a variety of subjects loosely tied to an alternately shamefaced and boastful account of the sexual adventures of a young poet, has in this later version become the reflections of a seasoned writer on sexual experience in general, and on his own adventures seen as stages not in his development as a lover, but as a writer.

Instead of the twenty-six texts of *Intermezzo di rime,* the new *Intermezzo* contains a total of fifty-two poems—most of them sonnets, as in the original collection, and all of them now with titles of their own. Not surprisingly, there are many references to the symbolist and decadent writers that had been important in the *Poema paradisiaco,* though now it is their wicked rather than langorous aspects that are emphasized. In the new group of sonnets on famous adulteresses, for example, D'Annunzio indulges his taste for the scandalous and prurient mixed with a free reading of history and legend, in his contamination of sacred and erotic following the lead of such decadents as Gustave Flaubert in his *Tentation de Saint Antoine* and Oscar Wilde, whose *Salomé* had been published in Paris the previous year. Even though *Intermezzo's* new structure is meant to encourage its interpretation as a story of debauchery followed by repentance, many of the new poems suggest a greater enthusiasm for the delights of the former than for the strictures of the latter. In some of them the sexual content takes a decidedly misogynous and sadistic turn. In "Godoleva," for example, one of D'Annunzio's "adulteresses" is punished by an irate husband who thrusts a flaming torch into that part of his wife's body that he believes has offended him most, leaving it afterwards "a smoldering and shapeless cavern." As this detail indicates, if anything, the revised *Intermezzo* is more pornographic than *Intermezzo di rime* had ever been.

Perhaps the most important addition to the 1894 *Intermezzo* is its "Preludio" (Prelude), in effect D'Annunzio's authorized interpretation of the entire volume and of his career to date. Its nearly 150 terza rima lines are a first-person description of the poet as hero, following the Pegasus of poetic inspiration across a perilous sea on a course marked for him by such illustrious predecessors as Ulysses, Dante, and Tasso's Rinaldo. Landing in a fragrant garden reminiscent of the *Poema paradisiaco,* the young and inexperienced traveler is set upon by dangerous damsels whose "bloodless hands," "ardent mouths," and deep familiarity with "tutte le belle cose impure" (all the beautiful, impure things) threaten to unman him. In due time, one of them does "take pleasure in the Adolescent," but only to disappear afterward, leaving him alone to reflect on his poetic mission. Despite his misadventures in this initial poem, by the end of *Intermezzo* the poet is ready to set sail again. In its concluding "Commiato" (Envoy) he vows to abandon the "shame" and "dead pleasures" of both an erotic and poetic sort. "My heart dreams," he says in lines that echo similar sentiments already quoted from "Vespro," "of a grander life / and a fiercer death. / Sing, o winds! In the unknown Sea / lies the promised Island. / There, as if upon an immense altar / lies the promised Glory. / I will stamp the mark of my boot upon it. / Promised glory, you are mine!"

In this poem D'Annunzio insists on the essential unity of erotic and heroic activity—an important theme throughout his career that in this volume receives explicit exposition in the paired sonnets, "Erotica-Heroica." D'Annunzio's most distinguished French critic has acutely remarked that the title of this work "could serve for all of [D'Annunzio's] writing." "In this period more than ever," Professor Tosi continues, "heroism—that is, what he calls heroism—has its roots in eroticism, in sexual excess. More than ever, woman is the enemy—the indispensable Enemy—of the hero, of the superman."[8] While D'Annunzio's notions about the equivalence of sexual and political mastery will be explored more fully in the novels of the early 1890s, in these poems it is already clear how important the influence of Nietzsche has been for him. In the highly idiosyncratic interpretation of the German philosopher's thought that D'Annunzio was beginning to develop in this period, the artist is the supreme example of the *Uebermensch* or Superman. Even such a tacky, if flamboyant, member of this category as the emperor Nero is thus worthy of admiration. In "Qualis artifex pereo!" Nero, whose last act was supposed to have been to "fiddle while Rome burned," is presented as a model of the exceptional individual intent on creating a "magnificent life" who died weeping for "Art alone!" Significantly, the phrase (Nero's supposed last utterance) that provides the title for this poem began to appear during this same period on D'Annunzio's private stationery, though with the "Qualis artifex *pereo*" (I die as an artist) of the original now changed to "Qualis artifex *valeo*" (I flourish as an artist).[9]

In the new narrative organization of his older poetry in *Intermezzo* D'Annunzio is preparing the way for the more consistently narrative *Laudi,* especially *Alcyone.* His major concern at the moment, however, is to assign a meaning to his previous artistic and biographical experience by inserting it into the larger story of the emergence of Gabriele D'Annunzio as exceptional being, every bit of whose life is of the greatest interest not only to himself as simultaneous protagonist and amanuensis of this adventure, but also to the public he knows is eagerly awaiting enlightenment about it.

The 1896 *Canto novo*

In 1896, two years after the revised *Intermezzo*, D'Annunzio brought out a new edition of *Canto novo*, this time with Treves in Milan. The new collection contains only twenty-seven poems as compared to sixty-three in 1882, and the texts are now grouped into two sections instead of the original five. "Canto del sole" (Song of the sun) and "Canto dell' Ospite" (Song of the guest) contain twelve poems each, most of them from the original edition but rewritten for the occasion. Three new compositions, all with the identical title of "Offerta votiva" (Votive offering), appear at the beginning, between the two sections, and at the conclusion of the volume. In addition, all references to Elda Zucconi have disappeared as have the sonnets of social protest.

By the time he revised *Canto novo* D'Annunzio was not only the author of several additional books of poetry, he had also made a madcap and poetically stimulating trip to Greece, and had come into contact with the thought of Nietzsche. D'Annunzio's encounter with the ideas of the German philosopher had immediate and profound effects on the novels of this period, especially the *Trionfo della morte* of 1892 and *Le vergini delle rocce* of 1895; more will be said about this matter in the analysis of them to follow. But Nietzsche's influence can be seen in the new *Canto novo* too, especially in this volume's conception of the poet as someone fated for exceptional experiences. The many stylistic changes made to the new volume, many of which seem to have been inspired by the poet's increased familiarity with contemporary French poetry, also make the new volume a more distinctly and subtly musical work than the rough-hewn 1882 original.

The first "Offerta votiva" of the new *Canto novo* is a hymn to Venus in which the poet describes the smashing of his study lamp on that goddess's altar—a farewell to the sterile erudition of "pallid foreheads bending over pallid books." From now on, he proclaims, he will turn to the "burning deity" of the sun for light and illumination. In the 1882 original this poem had dealt with convalescence from a slight illness; in the new version all references to illness have disappeared in an emphasis on the "gushings of life" that "gurgle red" within the narrator in response to the rays of what in 1882 had been a "gentle sun" but is now a "burning divinity."

Sun and sea also dominate the fourth poem of the "Canto del sole," in which the narrator sets out in a small boat into a dawn so beautiful it seems a goddess with whom he longs to "couple in joyous union."

However, the sunrise soon invests the scene with such sparkling light and color that the poet's heart and nerves begin to tremble before "the immense poem of all things" his verse has created and a voice within him cries out that perhaps he has been transformed into a god. Later on he dreams again of metamorphosis into a divinity, this time during an encounter with a wood nymph. In the 1882 version of this poem he had hoped only that this nymph would "suck the flower of his youth" in sexual congress; now he begs her to let him live "like a powerful god within his fable." The final poem of this section describes another encounter with a god who this time moves within the poet in such a way that the "eternal pulsation of the World" begins to beat in tune with his heart, and his body is magically changed into a tree-bearing island that seafarers gaze at in wonder.

After a votive offering to the god Pan, the "Song of the Guest" continues with twelve more poems set at the sea, though more frequently during the night or early morning and in a gentler tone than previously. In one of these the poet's body is again transformed when he wakes after a night of love to find himself turned into a tree. As this "divine tree extends its previously unseen power into the motionless air," his lady sings to him "as if in a fable"—another fantasy of corporeal aggrandizement, increased sexual potency, and narcissistic satisfaction. The volume ends with praise to Apollo, god of the sun and of poetry.

In the new *Canto novo* D'Annunzio has composed a tightly narrated book of lyric poetry in a symbolic landscape dense with classical reminiscences. His encounter with primitive though literarily mediated natural forces has enabled him not so much to discover the elemental world of the senses (the case, instead, for the first edition of this collection) as to recognize his own exceptional importance as the hero of a "fable" of immense significance.

Chapter Three
Experiments in Fiction: The Life and Death of the Novel

During the late 1880s and early 1890s when D'Annunzio was refining his poetic skills through continued exercise in this genre and careful study of French poetry, he was also writing novels. Eventually, there would be seven of these, most of them from the decade between 1889 and 1899, though his last work of this kind was not published until 1910. While other Italian novelists of the period often turned to the past for their subjects or wrote about characters different from themselves in social class, age, sex, temperament, and so on, all of D'Annunzio's writings of this sort have contemporary settings and principal characters who are in one way or another projections of their author's own personality.[1] For the most part, D'Annunzio's novels are narratively static affairs, more sounding boards for his ideas and showcases for his prose style than complex narrative structures in the manner of a Dickens, a Balzac, or a Manzoni.

Il piacere

D'Annunzio's first novel is *Il piacere* (*The Child of Pleasure*, 1898); it was published by Treves in 1889. Although he was able to utilize a good deal of his previous experience and even of his previous published writing in it, D'Annunzio found he could not finish the novel while working full-time as a newspaper reporter and he quit his job at Count Sciarra's *Tribuna,* the last regular salaried job of this sort he was ever to hold, in order to complete it. Retiring to his friend Francesco Paolo Michetti's villa in the Abruzzi, he wrote the entire work in five months of concentrated effort in the summer and fall of 1888.

The 1880s that serve as background for *Il piacere* were a time of political and social crisis for the still-fledgling Italian state. Although it treats them only in passing, the novel contains several references to such critical issues of the day as public demonstrations by the increasingly organized Italian workers, the failure of Italy's colonial adventures in Africa, and—in the episode of the sickly baby whom the protagonists Elena and Andrea encounter in its first chapter—the country's lamentable public health conditions.

However, although one critic has spoken of *Il piacere* as a novel of crisis both for D'Annunzio personally and for an era whose "lack of ideals and desperate hedonism" it depicts,[2] this is not a work that deals with social issues, even if it is more fully developed sociologically than any of D'Annunzio's other novels. As its title indicates, *Il piacere* is principally an examination of pleasure, especially of a sensual and sexual sort: a study, as its author says in his dedication to Michetti, of "corruption . . . depravity . . . vain ingenuity, falseness and cruelty." In this book D'Annunzio is no longer dealing with a bestial sexuality of the sort described in his Abruzzi stories, but is concerned instead with the refined eroticism of city dwellers for whom sex is not just one more powerful emotion like hunger, greed, or rage, but a potentially all-consuming passion that often seems to constitute their sole reason for living.

Il piacere is the story of a few months in the life of the dashing man-about-Rome Count Andrea Sperelli, a character the novel's readers had little difficulty in recognizing as a fictional representation of D'Annunzio himself. As the book opens, this "last descendant of an intellectual race" and a man determined to live his life as though he were creating a work of art, is expecting a visit from Elena Muti, a beautiful and amorously enthusiastic Roman duchess. The first pages of the work describe the care Andrea has devoted to setting the scene for this encounter. As he arranges roses in crystal vases like those in a famous Botticelli painting, the flowers "seem to present an image of a religious or amorous offering," a contamination of the sacred with the erotic reminiscent of certain pages of *La Chimera*. Andrea is taking "special, affectionate care" with the details in the room because he is a "delicate stage performer" who cannot "comprehend love's comedy without a scenario."[3] Sperelli's spectacular success as a lover, in fact, is the result of his chameleonlike character, his ability to combine "within him something of Don Giovanni and of Cherubino: he knew how to be the man of a Herculean night and a timid, sincere, almost virginal lover . . . in the art of love, he felt no repugnance toward any fiction, any falseness, any lie. A large part of his strength lay in hypocrisy" (*Romanzi*, 1.14). Histrionic as well as hypocritical, Andrea often acts out the roles he has set for himself so successfully that distinctions between his fictive and real desires and personalities become lost in the process. Not unlike D'Annunzio himself, perhaps, Andrea Sperelli seems to have no identity of his own other than the tendentious representations of self that he is constantly creating in his fictions.

As the story of *Il piacere* unfolds, the count finds himself face to face with certain recalcitrant and unpleasant aspects of reality. First Elena leaves him for an emotionally painful but financially expedient marriage; then Andrea himself is wounded in a fatuously instigated duel. Convalescing afterward at his sister's villa, he decides to renounce the empty pleasures that have been such an important part of his old way of life for the less transient and more satisfying joys of art. While with his sister, he also initiates a second love affair with the beautiful but reserved Maria Ferres, the Sienese wife of a Guatemalan diplomat and the mother of a little girl. By the time Andrea's convalescence is complete, this spiritualized counterpart to the ardent Elena has fallen completely in love with him. But once his wounds are healed and he has returned to Rome, Andrea quickly forgets both Maria and his good intentions and throws himself into dissipation once more. In the midst of these frolics he again encounters Elena, by now the wife of an English lord of repulsive manner and odious sexual proclivities. Caught as he is between the spiritual Maria and the besmirched but still-irresistible Elena, Andrea decides to fashion a third, ideal mistress in his mind's eye by thinking about the sexy Elena while making love to Maria, whom he has by now seduced. But in a culminating scene he ruins everything by pronouncing Elena's name during just such a moment. At the end of the book, Andrea finds himself abandoned by both women, alone and disconsolate in a Rome where the cultural and artistic values that are so important to him are slowly perishing before the onslaught of an indifferent and vulgarly materialistic civilization.

Stylistically, *Il piacere* is a remarkably successful tour de force. Not only is it one of D'Annunzio's most structurally coherent novels, but its carefully cadenced, poetic prose often rises to real lyric heights, as in the work's initial paragraph describing a golden December evening in Piazza di Spagna. A good bit of this opening page, whose first sentence is a perfect hendecasyllable line of Italian verse, is a reworking of one of *La Chimera*'s more successful rondeaux, and the entire novel is peppered with intertextual references to works by sculptors, painters, and writers that, of course, include D'Annunzio himself. In the allusions to his own works—to the *Elegie romane* for the Roman setting, the

Poema paradisiaco for the aura of languor and "goodness" during Andrea's convalescence, as well as to *La Chimera*—D'Annunzio is indulging in a kind of "second degree mannerism" that has been remarked as one of the constants of his style in both prose and poetry throughout his career.[4]

In addition to its glossy and attractive stylistic surface, *Il piacere* is jammed with fashionable objects. Some of these are the actual works of art, bibelots, and bric-a-brac that crowd its interiors and that its characters are so eager to buy at auction, talk about, and invest with symbolic meaning. Still other objects appear in the book's many valorizing metaphors comparing characters, settings, or objects to rarer or more famous exemplars from history or legend. Thus Andrea's vases in the opening scene already referred to are not only costly and unusual, they acquire an increased value through their capacity to recall similar vases in a priceless Botticelli painting.

Many of the material things that appear in the novel are utilized in a context different from that for which they were originally designed. This refunctionalization of such objects as the religious paraments Andrea uses to decorate the walls of his bachelor flat shows both a disdain for history as anything other than a source of aesthetic emotion and a tendency toward the fetishization of consumer goods in which the original use-value of the object is submerged in a new symbolic significance. The many objects so treated in this book take on new importance as the symbolically invested physical emanations of their owners' characters and taste. At the same time, the arbitrary assignment of an almost magical essence to such rare objects tends to reduce everything to which such meaning has not been assigned to an empty shell devoid of significance. Not only does ordinary reality become degraded when compared to an imagined counterpart heavy with aesthetic analogy, but even when this investment has taken place, the world and its inhabitants are quickly reified into precious but also lifeless museum exhibits. It is partly because he senses that he is an inhabitant of just such a museum that Andrea must seek physical sensation at all costs and that the last works of art presented in the book are Lord Heathfield's distressing pornography collection.

In D'Annunzio's own time Sperelli provided an attractive model for bourgeois readers eager to emulate the mannerisms of an Italian aristocracy now beginning to fade in economic importance but allied with them in the struggle to discredit working-class aspirations to social and economic parity. Throughout this novel the erotic is identified with the rare and the costly and seems to be reserved for the rich and/or aristocratic. For example, not only does Andrea take great pleasure in riding with Elena in an expensive carriage where the latest in heaters keeps her "tiny ducal feet" warm, his satisfaction at being with her in a place of comfort and intimacy is increased by the glimpses he catches of "obscure people" suffering in the chill and muddy streets outside the carriage windows (72).

But if D'Annunzio's polemic against all that is vulgar sometimes seems to include the bourgeoisie in the mob that was his principal target, his criticism did not disqualify this text for success with middle-class readers masochistically willing to endure a modicum of class excoriation along with the other titillations the novel provided. In this book, which an early reader is reputed to have praised as "smelling of sperm,"[5] there were plenty of scenes that could provide such titillation, among them a sickroom seduction and an episode of lovemaking in which every pore of Elena's body is depicted as a jealous mouth competing eagerly for Andrea's attention. For all this, Andrea is a remarkably passive lover, easily dominated by Elena as a *belle dame sans merci;* it is she, for example, who initiates their sickbed coupling.

This and the other elaborate and self-conscious seductions that constitute the center of interest of this novel take place against the background of the society activities of the *bel mondo romano* of the era. A significant feature of this milieu was the many auction sales consequent to the breaking up of great households of the time. In D'Annunzio's case, the end of an era signaled by these sales meant not just the replacement of one class with another, but also a disastrous decline of all that was most precious in Italian civilization. Andrea Sperelli is deeply offended by this crumbling of artistic values because in him "the aesthetic sense" is so powerful "that it had taken over for the moral sense" (40). When this aesthetic sense too is put at the service of a quest for an erotic ideal that Sperelli believes latent in a world emptied of both historical and aesthetic significance, he ends up defeated and an anachronism.

Giovanni Episcopo

D'Annunzio's next novel, *Giovanni Episcopo* of 1891 (*Episcopo & Company,* 1896), is a very different work from *Il piacere,* at least at first glance. Instead of a tale of "pleasure," it is a story of painful humiliation, both moral and physical. Instead of being set among the high life of Roman café society, it takes place in the lowest reaches of urban existence in a gray and anonymous nineteenth-century metropolis that is in fact Rome but could just as well be Stockholm, Berlin, or St. Petersburg. Above all, instead of revolving around the swashbuckling adventures of the fascinating Andrea Sperelli, the new work chronicles the ruin of the morbidly compliant and colorless Giovanni Episcopo. It is thus not surprising that in a recent synthesis and schematization of a master plot for all of D'Annunzio's novels, *Giovanni Episcopo* is treated as a variation from the norm and the "exception that confirms the rule" of this writer's usual novelistic practice.[6]

Yet if Giovanni Episcopo is in many ways the polar opposite of Andrea Sperelli, and his Rome of squalid boardinghouses, mean-spirited clerks, and cold-water flats the antiexistence that the pleasure-loving world of *Il piacere* opposes, Andrea and Giovanni, like many violent opposites, also share certain significant characteristics. Both men, for example, are deeply dissatisfied with the worlds in which they live. Andrea's reaction is the decadent and antirealistic one of constructing a counterreality rich with arcane significance and thus a superior alternative to ordinary life. Giovanni allows himself to be carried along by demeaning events as if through this abnegation of his will—but not of his protesting imagination, as is clear from the comments he makes throughout the book—he can somehow conquer the hateful environment around him.

Moreover, despite the vast differences in the sexual fortunes of these two characters, both Andrea and Giovanni are prey to the same obsession: the desire for an erotic partner who will combine the contradictory qualities of intense spirituality and profound and irremediable impurity, a woman simultaneously angel and whore. In *Il piacere* Andrea Sperelli veered dramatically from an affair with a partner of great erotic potency who did in effect sell herself in a mercenary marriage, to another with a woman of deep and almost angelic spirituality, in the end attempting unsuccessfully to combine both types in a third, imaginary woman evoked in his mind's eye while his body was occupied with one of the two original paradigms. Giovanni, somewhat differently, allows himself to marry a person who enjoys serving as the object of desire for all who see her, a woman who quickly proves a spectacularly unfaithful and sadistic wife and an unfeeling and incompetent mother. In his relationship with this woman the hero derives masochistic satisfaction not only from the inhuman treatment to which she subjects him, but also from her failure to live up to the elementary ideals of human decency that he keeps constantly before his moral imagination. Like

Sperelli, Episcopo projects the image of one sort of woman and behavior onto a sharply contrasting reality. If, on a social or political level, Giovanni Episcopo exists in order to make manifest the superiority of people like Andrea Sperelli, on the psychosexual level the two men's personalities are not quite so unlike as they might at first appear.

It has already been noted how in the first years of the 1890s D'Annunzio had come into contact with the novels of Tolstoy and Dostoyevski and *Giovanni Episcopo* has been described as an attempt to write a "Russian novel" in Italian. But even though the hero of this work undergoes a deep and crushing humiliation, Giovanni Episcopo is not transformed by the matters that lead up to his confession. Even though he is described as a "Christus patiens" in the book's introduction and compares himself to Christ at one point in the story, Giovanni has married Ginevra from physical desire, not out of a spirit of sacrifice; he endures being humiliated by her not because he is a Christ-like figure but because he is a weak one. If D'Annunzio has indeed been influenced by Dostoyevski in this novel, he has mis-understood or profoundly altered the Russian writer's message of re-demption through suffering. In the end Giovanni Episcopo has not been redeemed; he is merely defeated, the destiny of virtually all of the heroes of D'Annunzio's novels.

Giovanni Episcopo also represents an additional break with naturalism. Despite its scientific approach to an understanding of human behavior and pathology, the new novel has abandoned the objective attitudes of "veristic" narrative. From beginning to end *Giovanni Episcopo* is a first-person confession in which Giovanni explains how he entered into a loveless marriage that produced a beloved son but also led to his increasing humiliation and final ruin when he killed his wife's lover after the lover had struck Giovanni's child. The effect of this confession is to encourage reflection on the extraordinary psychological constitution of the title character and on human psychology in general. Even if its clinical concern for aberrant types like Giovanni, Wanzer, and Ginevra is typical of much naturalist writing in Italy or France, *Giovanni Episcopo*'s confessional dimension places it closer to the writings of such psychological novelists as Paul Bourget than to the contemporary experiments of a naturalist like Zola.

In the important dedicatory letter to Matilde Serao that accompanied *Giovanni Episcopo* beginning with the Pierro edition of 1892, D'Annunzio expresses "shame and rage" at certain passages in a "book of prose" that can only be *Il piacere,* going on to assert that in his writing from now on he will "study people and things DIRECTLY and without intermediaries." His slogan from this time forward, he continues, will be "o rinnovarsi o morire" (either renew oneself or die). However, although Giovanni's masochism in this work is a psychological attitude usually reserved for D'Annunzio's women characters, in other ways the hero of this novel is unlike D'Annunzio's more glamorous male figures only in that he knows he is defeated at the beginning of the novel and does not have to wait for its conclusion for his final debacle. Like many of D'Annunzio's other principal characters, Giovanni often complains that "a sense of reality escaped [him]" (*Romanzi*, 2.351). But what ties this figure in D'Annunzio's least successful novel most closely to the rest of this author's work is his reflection on the real motives for human activity: "Every man nourishes a secret dream within him that is neither goodness nor love, but the unbridled desire for pleasure and egoism," says Giovanni Episcopo. "No human creature loves any other human creature or has ever been loved by another human creature. I have never dared to confess this horrid truth to myself for fear of dying from it" (361). Many years later, at a time when he could feel himself sliding down the precipitous decline of old age to immanent death, D'Annunzio expressed similar sentiments in this bitter jingle:

> Tutta la vita è senza mutamento.
> Ha un solo volto la malinconia.
> Il pensiere ha per cima la follia.
> E l'amore è legato al tradimento.
> (*Prose*, 2. 926)
> [All of life is monotony.
> Melancholy has just one face.
> Madness is thought's highest place.
> And love is bound to treachery.]

This reprise of sentiments articulated many years earlier by one of his weakest and most antiheroic literary figures indicates both how perennial these dark sentiments were in D'Annunzio's system of thought and how much even such a character as Giovanni Episcopo shares with his creator's most secret thoughts.

L'Innocente

The hero of D'Annunzio's next novel, *L'Innocente* (1892, in English as *The Intruder*, 1897) bears a greater resemblance to Andrea Sperelli than he does to Giovanni Episcopo—even though *L'Innocente* is meant to be a further step in the "renovation" of D'Annunzio's art set out in the dedicatory letter to Serao. A "family romance" especially concerned with the issues of love, reproduction, and paternity that are so important in his fiction of the early and middle 1890s, *L'Innocente* was written in three months during the spring and summer of 1891. D'Annunzio had hoped to place the manuscript with Treves, the house that had published *Il piacere* and would very soon be bringing out both the *Poema paradisiaco* and the *Trionfo della morte*. But Emilio Treves did not like *L'Innocente*, which he found "highly immoral"—a mixture, as he put it, of Tolstoy and the Marquis de Sade.[7] Fortunately for D'Annunzio, his friends Serao and Scarfoglio took a different view of the work, and agreed to publish it in the *Corriere di Napoli*, a daily Neapolitan newspaper they were managing. Between December 1891 and February 1892 *L'Innocente* came out in installments in the *Corriere*. Shortly afterward it was published as a book by Bideri in Naples, dedicated in this form to Maria Gravina. Treves eventually had second thoughts about the novel, bought up the rights, and in 1896 reissued it as the second (after *Il piacere*) of "I romanzi della Rosa" (Novels of the rose).

Although the book's early reception in Italy was somewhat tepid, possibly because Italian readers tended to agree with Treves about the work's "immorality," *L'Innocente* was a hit when it appeared in translation in France. The first of D'Annunzio's novels to be published in that country, *L'Intrus* (The intruder), as the French version was called, was an immediate favorite with both the reading public and the critics, who praised its author as a "Latin with a Slavic soul." Its commercial and critical success mark the beginning of D'Annunzio's considerable fame outside Italy as well as of his collaboration with his most important French translator, Georges Hérelle. A Cherbourg philosophy teacher who had come across the novel in its serialized version, Hérelle was to become D'Annunzio's principal translator in France, and a collaborator and close friend.[8]

D'Annunzio's *L'Innocente* is the story of an infanticide. It is told in the first person by Tullio Hermil, a well-to-do landowner who glories in his success at being "constantly unfaithful to a constantly faithful woman" (*Romanzi*, 1.412). The woman in question is his adoring wife, Giuliana. As the novel opens, Tullio, like the narrator of the *Poema paradisiaco,* has decided to renounce his life of debauchery and seek spiritual renewal in the purity of the family bosom. He is quickly forced to alter this plan, however, when he discovers that the neglected Giuliana has herself given in to a "moment of weakness" with the writer Filippo Arborio and is now pregnant with Arborio's child. Tullio cannot bear the thought of this "maleficent little being" intruding into his family and, with Giuliana's connivance, he does away with the infant by exposing it to a draft of winter air from an open window. The novel ends with the funeral of this innocent victim.

Like Andrea Sperelli, Tullio Hermil considers himself an exceptional man, a person "different from others and [with] a different conception of life," able "to avoid the duties others would like to impose" and "rightly to scorn other people's opinions and live out his chosen nature with absolute candor" (372). Also like Sperelli, Tullio finds himself caught between two women, the dark and doting Giuliana and the blonde and passionate Teresa Raffo ("Could there be a blonder, a more fascinating, a more desirable woman than she in Rome?" [395]). While the vampire Teresa excites a passion in Tullio that flings him into the darkest depths of sexual degradation,[9] Giuliana occupies the opposite pole in his sadomasochistic dynamic. Ready for any kind of abnegation, she is willing to serve as "friend, sister, wife, mistress, forever ready for any sacrifice for [his] pleasure's sake" (525). Although Giuliana is a diaphanously beautiful woman, with skin "whiter than her blouse," she is also the possessor of reproductive organs that Tullio views "with terrifying lucidity" as "the primal sore, the filthy wound forever open that bleeds and stinks" (384). Simultaneously a nonvirgin, even an adulteress, as well as a mother, Giuliana is both "impure" and the epitome of purity. Tullio's attitude toward her is thus a contradictory mixture of sadistic hatred and filial devotion, though he is deeply pleased when, during their lovemaking, Giuliana, "Beside herself and with a strangled voice, crie[s] out, "Yes, yes—kill me!'" (543). Even though he finds such feelings deplorable, Tullio is convinced of the ubiquity of his sadistic urges. "Why is there this horrible faculty in man's nature of enjoying himself more intensely when he knows he is hurting the creature from which he is deriving pleasure," he asks himself. "Why, in every man who loves and desires, does there lie the germ of such an abominable sadistic perversion?" (393–94). But what bothers Tullio more than these feelings, more even than his dismay at the simultaneously pure and impure nature of such women as Giuliana, is his frustration at the recalcitrance of reality to be manipulated by human will and desire. It is this that causes him to burst into tears that leave him "exhausted . . . dried out, more convinced than ever of his own impotence, physically dazed and depressed by this confrontation with impassible reality" (533).

Tullio's problem in this novel concerns the nature and limits of paternal responsibility—a matter that was causing D'Annunzio no little difficulty in his private life during this period of his relationship with Maria Gravina. In the novel the unwanted child is christened "Raimondo," both Tullio's father's name and an appellation whose diminutive, "Mondino" (a term by which he is also called in the novel), can also mean "pure." That the child has this name suggests that Raimondo is both an infantile representation of Tullio's father and an impurely conceived but nonetheless innocent being who in this way shares the contradictory nature of his pure and impure mother. Tullio's murder, therefore, of his father's namesake, alter ego's offspring, and replication of his wife's distressingly double nature can be understood as a rejection not just of this multiply significant child, but also of a confusing and alienating fatherhood that threatens to diminish his own ego.[10] L'Innocente, in this reading, is a modern version not of the story of Oedipus but of the counter tale of Oedipus's father Laius who, forseeing the threat that Oedipus posed to his kingdom and marriage bed, determined to kill his son and rival before this could happen. While in the original myth it was the father who was killed, here Oedipus himself has been suppressed by a modern Laius struggling to keep all of the mother figure's love for himself. Like many of D'Annunzio's sexually independent heroines, Giuliana suffers from a gynecological malady, and before her encounter with Arborio has undergone a surgical procedure to correct this malaise. But from Tullio's perspective, Raimondo is the ultimate gynecological infection. Once this infection has been removed through his death, this mark of Giuliana's impurity can be erased and she can return to the condition of health and wholesomeness that prevailed before her contamination.

However considered, Tullio's murder of Raimondo does not—at least in his view—make him liable to the ordinary code of criminal justice. Where the epigraph of Giovanni Episcopo was the biblical: "Judica me secundum justitiam tuam" (Judge me according to your justice), Hermil states explicitly on the opening page of L'Innocente that "the justice of men cannot touch me. No court on earth would know how to judge me." Tullio's gesture, therefore, is a "crime of honor" like that committed by Compar Alfio when he discovers Santuzza's unfaithfulness in Verga's story (and later Mascagni's opera) Cavalleria rusticana.[11] In Verga's tale, however, it is Turiddu rather than Santuzza who is made to pay the price for their adulterous love. In D'Annunzio's tale of middle-class rather than peasant chivalry, adultery is wrong, but especially wrong for women. Those women who do insist on sexual independence are swiftly punished for "moments of weakness" by infections of their reproductive organs and ultimate loss of their children. Security lies only within the family circle, whose members—especially the mother and the deceased sister, who here has the significant name Costanza (Constance)—take on the status of secular saints as reward for their unflagging support of their frequently transgressing men. In this charmed circle an "Intruder" of any sort must be resented as "different" and "other" just as non-Italians will be seen as "other" in D'Annunzio's later and more overtly racist fiction and political declamations.

While *L'Innocente* does not constitute a liberation from the middle-class mores that continued to vex D'Annunzio in both his fiction and his personal life, in terms of style the novel represents a real advance over *Giovanni Episcopo*. Instead of the flat and deliberately insipid writing of that work, the new book features a musical, cadenced prose reminiscent of the best pages of *Il piacere*. Even though much of it is given over to descriptions of painful psychological experiences, the external world depicted by this novel is often a world of great beauty: the beauty of sunlight, of curtains moving gently in a summer's breeze, of the smells of a fine day, of a small girl sleeping, of the clear, white skin of a beautiful woman, of a flower-filled garden at a country villa. If *L'Innocente* is one of D'Annunzio's better novels, this is perhaps not so much because of its lurid and impacted plot, but because of the ductile, lucid, and beautiful language in which its unhappy and finally unresolved story is cast.[12]

Trionfo della morte

D'Annunzio's obsession with purity and impurity in sexual and reproductive matters is even more marked in his next novel, *Trionfo della morte* (*Triumph of Death*, 1896)[13] of 1894. The most composite of all of his longer prose fictions, it was begun shortly after *Il piacere* and just before *Giovanni Episcopo* and *L'Innocente*. Between January and March 1890, parts of it appeared as *L'Invincibile* (The invincible) in installments in the Roman *Tribuna illustra* (Illustrated Tribune), though it was never completed with this title. D'Annunzio had begun to think about the novel as early as March 1889, well before his military service and at a time when his passion for Barbara Leoni was

at its most incandescent. Like the *Elegie romane,* some of whose lines
are echoed in its pages, it can be read as both homage to Barbara and
an attempt by its author to exorcise this woman from his life and
literary imagination. Sometime after his discharge from the army in
November 1890, D'Annunzio took up the work again, reorganized,
completed, and retitled it; beginning in 1893, the *Trionfo della morte*
began to appear in *Il mattino* of Naples. Treves published it in a
volume the following year, later including it as the third of the "Romanzi
della rosa."

By 1894, D'Annunzio had not only written several volumes of fiction
and poetry, he had also come under the spell of Nietzsche. This crucial
encounter had an important effect on the *Trionfo della morte* and was
to have a still greater impact on his even more overtly Nietzschean
next novel, *Le vergini della rocce* (1895: *Maidens of the Rocks,* 1898),
and on all of his subsequent writing. At the end of the preface to the
Trionfo della morte D'Annunzio pays tribute to "the voice of the
magnanimous Zarathustra," and explicitly characterizes his new work
as preparation for the arrival of an *Uebermensch* or Superman (*Romanzi,*
1.658). In this same preface he insists that the apparent formlessness
of his novel is the result of an attempt "not to imitate but to continue
nature." While the *Trionfo della morte* may not have "the continuity
of a well-made plot" (the plot, it may be remembered, was "the soul"
of a work of art for the mimetic critic Aristotle but a much less crucial
element of expression for the free-ranging Nietzsche), it does have "the
continuity of an individual existence as it manifests itself over a certain
period of time" (654).

Although the structure of the *Trionfo della morte* was probably
determined more by the way it happened to be written (a process first
interrupted for a long time that then took more than five years to
accomplish) than by prior authorial notions of novelistic form, D'Annunzio is here claiming that his recent work constitutes a new fictional
type. In his view the *Trionfo della morte* is different from other Italian
writing of the era not only because of its devaluation of plot, but also
because of its blend of lyric and narrative modalities into a new expressive
synthesis. The result is "an ideal modern book . . . a work of beauty
and of poetry, of plastic and symphonic prose, rich in images and in
music" (654). In creating this music, D'Annunzio points out that he
has used a much larger vocabulary than is usually the case. Not only
do many of his contemporary prose writers use too few words, he goes
on, many of these words are not really Italian, but have an "impure

origin" or have been "deformed by a vulgar usage that has displaced or altered their original meaning" (655). In this preface D'Annunzio is associating his new novel with Nietzsche's philosophy, defending the apparent formlessness of his book as willed rather than accidental, and enunciating a kind of lexicological nationalism in which the already-familiar notion of antagonism between the pure and the impure has been extended from the social-sexual to the lexical and artistic realm.

Like *Il piacere, Giovanni Episcopo,* and *L'Innocente, Trionfo della morte* is the story of a failure, or rather a series of failures. As it begins, Giorgio Aurispa is seeking to give some meaning to his life and to establish a more psychologically satisfying relationship with his mistress, Ippolita Sanzio. When family concerns take him on a visit to his birthplace in the Abruzzi, Giorgio recognizes how different he has become from the other members of his family and realizes that he can no longer be of much use to them in resolving their existential problems or financial difficulties. When he later slips away with Ippolita for an extended country idyll, their unrestrained lovemaking is tainted by his awareness of Ippolita's unyielding alterity even at those moments when she seems to be giving herself to him most unreservedly. Painfully aware of his alienation from both his family and his mistress, Giorgio begins to think of Ippolita as "la Nemica" or "the Enemy," and to view her as a threat to his own existence.

While in the country with Ippolita, Giorgio is also struck by the vigor of the peasants who live around them, people from whose stock he has himself sprung, and whose authenticity and vitality he finds characteristic of a superior race. But when he and Ippolita join a pilgrimage to a rustic sanctuary in the distant village of Casalbordino, his admiration for the simple people of the region quickly turns to revulsion. In a famous episode Giorgio and Ippolita are set upon by a grotesque assemblage of filthy and ignorant beggars and invalids abjectly seeking a miraculous cure from menacing powers they hold in superstitious awe. This is not the sturdy pre-Christian peasant religion that Giorgio had imagined earlier, nor are these the superior beings he had thought to find in this rustic setting. Casalbordino thus marks the end of his populist and racist notions of identification with the people of his native region.

Furthermore, Giorgio is by now increasingly repelled by Ippolita, whose sexual enthusiasm he finds intimidating, imagining her womb to be "a burning furnace" where "every seed must perish" (942). In such circumstances, sexual contact between the two becomes increasingly distressing. Finally, after a scene in which he is either unwilling or unable to satisfy Ippolita's sexual demands except by a proxy maneuver that induces first orgasmic convulsions, and then uncontrollable laughter, Giorgio hurls both himself and his struggling companion off a cliff and into the sea in a final *Liebestod* inspired by (even if not quite congruent with) Wagner's *Tristan und Isolde*. Death the invincible has triumphed over this protagonist's unsuccessful attempts to establish communication with an entity beyond the limits of his own ego, whether this be a family or other collectivity, a religion or ideology, or simply another human being.

The *Trionfo della morte* is a more explicitly autobiographical novel than either *Giovanni Episcopo* or *L'Innocente*. D'Annunzio's stormy relationship with his father, for example, is clearly the model for Giorgio Aurispa's troubling encounter with his father and the doubling of this "bad" paternal image by the "good" Uncle Demetrio, who Giorgio at one point says "was my real father" (877), shows how alienated D'Annunzio was from his own father, whose funeral in June 1893 he did not even attend. To round out this oedipal symmetry, Giorgio's mother is positively portrayed as a good but suffering woman who must be protected from a vicious husband, a woman whose jealousy of Ippolita makes even clearer the exclusionist nature of her demands on her son's affections. As already mentioned, Ippolita Sanzio is closely based on Barbara Leoni, some of the poet's actual letters to her even being utilized verbatim in the novel's text. To an unusual degree, then, the *Trionfo della morte* is a kind of psychodrama or fictional projection of certain crucial issues in D'Annunzio's own psychic history.[14] Partly for this reason, the attitudes taken in it toward women and sexual relations are of particular interest. In *L'Innocente* the menacing "Other" was the unwanted baby whose presence threatened his putative father's monopoly over Giuliana's affection; in *Giovanni Episcopo* the title character was much too weak to hold his wife's affection or even very much of her attention. In the new novel it is Woman herself—as sexual partner but not as mother and without reference to a rival—who is Other and the enemy. Ippolita Sanzio, married to someone else and incapable of having a baby, is both sterile and impure, mutually reinforcing qualities connected to her strong sexual appetites which in turn derive from her working-class and therefore equally "impure" social origins. For Giorgio, Ippolita is "an instrument of base lasciviousness," of such contaminated origin that "nothing can change her substance, nothing can purify her. She has plebeian blood and in that blood who knows what ignoble legacies!" (1020). Although it is Ippolita rather than Giorgio who faints away at contact with the "horrors of human flesh" (902) at Casalbordino, it is Giorgio who afterward characterizes their own love as "bestial conjunction, copulation effected with excremental organs, [a] sad and sterile spasmodic act" (983–84)[15]—a clear indication that it is the male partner in this couple who has been most profoundly transformed by their experiences at the Sanctuary.

By extending his scope in this novel beyond the narrow domain of interpersonal and sexual relations, D'Annunzio has moved an additional step toward the articulation of a political ideology. The *Trionfo della morte* represents a new anti-Christian, antipopular, and antifeminist position[16] that he appears to have derived at least in part from Nietzsche. Giorgio Aurispa is unlike the heroes of D'Annunzio's two previous novels in that he is completely disinterested in guilt or redemption. Even though he fails in his attempt to transform himself from impotent narcissist into Superman, he is someone for whom, at least in his own eyes, everything is permitted. Although D'Annunzio has not been able to assimilate all of Nietzsche's complex philosophical message into his own artistic and political system, in the German philosopher's work he has found important support for the supremacist ideology he is beginning to formulate.[17]

The *Trionfo della morte* also marks the beginning of the dissolution of novelistic conventions that will characterize D'Annunzio's later work in this genre. The story, for example, is frequently interrupted by the insertion of peripheral material brought in without alteration from other sources. The letters to Barbara Leoni quoted at length and without changes in the episode of the Lake Albano excursion are one example of an interpolation of this sort. Even more striking instances are the long quotations from Nietzsche and the extensive paraphrase of Wagner's *Tristan und Isolde* toward the end of the work. Concomitant with Giorgio's sense that the world around him is falling to pieces in response to Ippolita's sexual desire ("As she moved closer to him, serpentine and insidious, stretching out alongside him on the reed mat, a world was dissolving within him" [944–45]), in the *Trionfo della morte* the structure of the traditional novel is itself crumbling beneath the impact of D'Annunzio's increasingly urgent political and ideological preoccupations.

Le vergini delle rocce

Much of the *Trionfo della morte* is a melancholy meditation on sexual enmity and sterility in an incoherent and threatening universe. In *Le vergini delle rocce* (1895: *Maidens of the Rocks,* 1898), published the following year, D'Annunzio attempts to fill the ideological void into which Giorgio Aurispa had tumbled at the conclusion of the earlier work. D'Annunzio's new novel is concerned with fecundity rather than sterility and features a protagonist who is not miserable or indecisive, but self-confident and imbued with a new sense of mission in a responsive universe that he believes to be an emanation of his own personality. *Le vergini delle rocce* is a pivotal work in D'Annunzio's novelistic production, both for the ideology it articulates and for the new anti-novelistic and antirealistic structure it displays.

The title of D'Annunzio's fifth novel is derived from Leonardo da Vinci's famous painting, *The Virgin of the Rocks,* which the writer probably knew in its Paris rather than London version.[18] Before its appearance in a Treves volume in 1895 *Le vergini delle rocce*—like many of D'Annunzio's other works of this sort—was serialized, in this case in the Roman journal, *Il convito* (The banquet), beginning in January 1895 with the magazine's first number. D'Annunzio was also on the staff of this nationalistic and antidemocratic publication. In the "Proemio" to its first issue he described the journal's determination "to save what is beautiful and ideal from the dark wave of vulgarity currently obscuring the privileged land where Leonardo created his imperious women and Michelangelo his unconquerable heroes." In this struggle *Il convito* would mobilize "the hidden capabilities of [our] race," including "the indestructible power of Beauty, the sovereign dignity of the spirit, the necessity for intellectual hierarchies," and "the efficacy of the Word" as utilized by intellectuals devoted to "military-like support of the cause of Intelligence versus the Barbarians" (*Prose,* 2.455, 456).

Le vergini delle rocce is concerned with the "imperious women" and "unconquerable heroes" that D'Annunzio saw in Leonardo's and Michelangelo's paintings. Its own hero, Claudio Cantelmo, is the first positive protagonist to appear in any novel by this writer. Untroubled by the psychological turmoil that had tended to incapacitate D'Annunzio's previous heroes, Cantelmo is a man with a threefold mission: to realize in himself "the perfect fullness of the Latin type," to "concentrate the purest essence of the universe into a unique and supreme work of art," and to father a superior human being (*Romanzi*, 2.430). In the novel, he devotes most of his attention to the last of these projects—the siring of an extraordinary infant, a messianic "Colui che deve venire" (He who must come) and King of Rome who will rule over a politically reorganized Italy with the traditional aristocracy once again in the ascendency and those responsible for the "dark wave of vulgarity" menacing Italian culture kept firmly in their place. To do this, Claudio must have a wife, and much of *Le vergini delle rocce* describes his attempt to find a woman worthy of this lofty task. But even though Claudio does locate three promising candidates in the daughters of a noble but decaying family at a moldering estate in southern Italy, at the novel's conclusion he is still a bachelor, the three "virgins of the rocks" are still untouched (the only instance in D'Annunzio's writings of sexual desire remaining unconsummated for the entire length of a novel), and "Superbambino" still little more than a gleam in Cantelmo's feverish eye. Nonetheless, D'Annunzio's earlier division of the female sex into sterile and impure (but immensely desirable) women on the one hand and sacred mothers (and sometimes sisters) on the other, has now been transcended. For the first time in his fiction a novel's hero is able to imagine a single individual as both woman and mother, even if he is still too bewildered to unite with such a creature.

Although Claudio Cantelmo is as much a failure at the end of his tale as the heroes of previous works were at the conclusions of theirs, D'Annunzio had apparently intended to continue Claudio's story beyond the limits of *Le vergini delle rocce*. D'Annunzio's plan, as he set it out in a letter to his friend Vincenzo Morello, was for a sequel in two additional volumes called *La grazia* (Grace) and *L'annunciazione* (Annunciation). All three works would then have formed the trilogy of the "Romanzi del giglio" or "Novels of the Lily." As far as one can tell from this description, the sequence of novels would have been devoted to an examination of the advantages of high-minded love just as his previous "Novels of the rose" (as D'Annunzio had begun to call *Il piacere*, *L'Innocente*, and the *Trionfo della morte*) had been concerned with the voluptuousness and pain of various sorts of illicit or at least ill-advised passion.[19] In the sequel Anatolia, the sister who rejects Claudio's proposal at the end of the first book, was to have died, while a second sister, Massimila, entered a convent, and the remaining sister, Violante, first went mad but then regained her sanity long enough to marry Claudio and give birth to his child before herself expiring. At the end of the final volume, then, only Claudio and the child would have been left, all three of the virgins having in various ways disappeared from the rocky landscape that served as background for their story.

As he appears in the first and only completed work of this projected trilogy, the chaste and marriage-bent Superman Claudio Cantelmo is an unusual addition to D'Annunzio's cast of sexually exuberant males. Although *Le vergini delle rocce* is told entirely in the first person, at its conclusion the narrator is still almost completely lacking in distinguishing personal traits. Rather than a character in his own right, Claudio Cantelmo in this novel is a mouthpiece for D'Annunzio's ideas and a neutral sensibility through which the author may filter his displays of verbal virtuosity in the many stylized set pieces sprinkled throughout the book.

One of the ideas articulated by Cantelmo at the beginning of book 1 of *Le vergini delle rocce* is central to the novel's structure and ideological message. On the first page of this section Cantelmo expresses his conviction that "the world is the representation of the thought and sensibility of a few superior men who have created and then amplified and adorned it in the course of time and who will continue to amplify and adorn it in the future. The world as it appears today," Cantelmo goes on, "is a magnificent gift granted by the many to the few, from the free to the enslaved, from those who think and feel to those constrained to labor" (404). Although there may be some doubt about the good faith of this brave proclamation,[20] Cantelmo's solipsistic positing of the world as nothing more than a mental construct dispels the problem of the alterity of the physical universe that had paralyzed D'Annunzio's previous protagonists and frees his most recent hero for action in a newly manipulable world. The novel that follows is the most political of all of D'Annunzio's writings of this sort.

In Cantelmo's description of the universe as the representation of the thought and sensibility of a few superior individuals, the influence of both Schopenhauer and Nietzsche is evident. But it was the latter thinker who had the deeper and more lasting influence on his art and thought. D'Annunzio first encountered Nietzsche's ideas during the spring or summer of 1892 and began immediately to revise his views on guilt, expiation, and redemption—notions that were of great importance in the "Russian" novels *Giovanni Episcopo* and *L'Innocente* but ideas for which Nietzsche had nothing but scorn. In the beginning at least, D'Annunzio's knowledge of Nietzsche was derived entirely from excerpts from the philosopher's writings that had appeared in French translation beginning in April 1892.[21]

D'Annunzio's first work in which the influence of Nietzsche is evident and important is an article that appeared in Scarfoglio's *Mattino* in September 1892. In "La bestia elettiva" or "The Electoral Animal" D'Annunzio notes how, despite what he calls Italy's "universal suffrage" (electoral suffrage was far from universal in Italy in 1892), the lot of the Italian working classes has not improved appreciably since feudal times, a situation he finds inevitable rather than deplorable. For D'Annunzio in this article, it makes no difference whether the entity holding power in Italy is "that of a tribune or that of a king, whether the privileged class is the nobility or a Parliamentary majority." Whoever is running the government, "the plebes will continue to be slaves condemned to suffer—whether in the shadow of feudal towers or in that of the feudal smokestacks of a modern factory."[22] For D'Annunzio, humanity can be sorted into two different classes that occupy different stations and enjoy different privileges in life. "For the superior class which has elevated itself through the pure energy of its own will, everything will be permitted, for the inferior, little or nothing will be permitted."[23]

Consistent with the views expressed in "La bestia elettiva," the ideal state described in *Le vergini delle rocce* is "an institution perfectly adapted to favoring the gradual elevation of a privileged class toward an ideal form of existence," a political entity whose function is to encourage "a new realm of force" that will "dominate the multitudes." Modern Italy's troubles, in Cantelmo's view, are due to the aristocracy's desertion of its proper role which has allowed the country to fall into the hands of greedy speculators without moral scruples or aesthetic taste. Cantelmo is shocked that some members of aristocratic families famous for "centuries of merry pillage and ostentatious patronage" (431) are now speculating in the stock market or in Roman housing projects that lie like "some sort of immense, whitish, life-destroying tumor stuck on to the old City's side" (432).

Similar diatribes against the tastelessness of the new age and especially of the building boom that was transfiguring Rome in the final decades of the nineteenth century had been present in D'Annunzio's writing since *Il piacere*. In *Le vergini delle rocce,* however, this disdain for a burgeoning materialism serves as a point of departure for the formulation of a new supremacist doctrine in which the necessity for political force exercised by an Italian elite is combined with an equally fervid devotion to the cult of beauty. When Claudio Cantelmo thinks back upon his own heroic ancestors, for example, he remembers them "for the beautiful wounds that they opened, the beautiful fires that they set, the beautiful cups that they emptied, the beautiful clothes that they wore, the beautiful horses that they broke, the beautiful women that they enjoyed—for all their slaughters, their intoxications, their magnificent gestures, and their lusts" (419). The new oligarchy that he envisions taking power is worthy of its task because its members "have preserved the most beautiful dreams, the most daring emotions, the most noble thoughts, the most imperious wishes" (534–35) of the past.

As is evident from these quotations, D'Annunzio's conception of the Superman differs from Nietzsche's in several important respects. First of all, the superior individual whose advent Cantelmo prophesies is primarily an aesthetic figure whose devotion to beauty and taste for violent sensual indulgence are essential parts of his character. Second, D'Annunzio assumes that such a person can arise only from within an Italian race that has demonstrated its artistic primacy (as distinct from an ability for government) across the centuries. While Nietzsche's notion of the birth of a Superman was probably a metaphorical depiction of a spiritual rebirth possible for any of his readers sufficiently daring to face the implications of his thought, in *Le vergini delle rocce* D'Annunzio seems to be invoking an actual birth, and one that is possible only in certain racially circumscribed circumstances. Finally, where Nietzsche's concept of the exceptional human was antibourgeois and anticonventional, in the final analysis D'Annunzio's Superman tends to reinforce dominant bourgeois conventions. The political views that Cantelmo articulates in this novel were not at all out of line with other reactionary positions held by the Italian middle classes in late nineteenth-century Italy, a time that had seen not only the formation of the Italian socialist movement, but a powerful reaction to potential socialist hegemony through a turn to the Right in Italian politics, especially under Crispi, whose antipopulist policies at home and increasingly imperialistic tendencies abroad are typical of this era. In its historical context *Le vergini delle rocce* provided an artistic and pseudophilosophical apology for positions already assumed by a middle-class readership whose political views were shaped more by fear of the mob and uncertainty about their own position in the class system than by notions of innate superiority.

In this novel D'Annunzio turns away from the moralism and psychologism of his earlier fiction to a reliance on style alone as the principal bearer of his message. Although Claudio Cantelmo does not father the "Superbambino" and future King of Rome he is hoping for, he does become the author of an autonomous and nonmimetic superstyle. If,

as Cantelmo claims, the world is the representation of the thought and
sensibility of a few superior individuals, then a novel written by one
of these exceptional individuals has no representational responsibilities
and can assume any form its creator desires. In Cantelmo's novel
D'Annunzio has created a new antirealistic narrative structure in which
verisimilitude—whether of dialogue, characterization, action, setting, or
any of the other categories of traditional novelistic representation—is
submerged in the boiling reagent of D'Annunzio's most emphatic and
heated writing, until the traditional novelistic categories give way to an
oratorical and apocalyptic mode that is completely new in the history
of novelistic representation in Italy.

Il fuoco

Although D'Annunzio began writing his next novel shortly after
completing *Le vergini delle rocce*, *Il fuoco* (*The Flame of Life*, 1900)
was not published until 1900, almost five years later. There were several
reasons for this. For one thing, between 1895 and 1900 D'Annunzio
was extremely busy with a variety of activities. In 1895 he took a trip
to Greece with Edoardo Scarfoglio and others on Scarfoglio's yacht.
Although during this cruise D'Annunzio and friends spent at least some
of their time on shore sampling opportunities for misbehavior, they also
visited several classical sites and the trip as a whole had a significant
influence on the longtime Hellenophile's future poetry and writing for
the stage. In 1898 and 1899 D'Annunzio's first plays—one of which
had a classical setting—were performed. In 1896 there was a new
edition of *Canto novo,* and toward the end of the period he began to
write some of the poems later to be collected in the *Laudi.* The final
years of the century also saw the composition of the first of his
memorialistic *Faville dal maglio* or "Sparks from the Anvil," and in
1897 he ran successfully for a seat in Parliament. Most important of
all, during this same five-year period D'Annunzio became involved in
a major love affair, this time with the actress and international diva
Eleonora Duse. Duse was one of the most celebrated theatrical talents
of the day. Her tempestuous and relatively long-lived affair with the
Italian writer took place to a large extent in the public eye and had
important effects on the careers of both the personalities involved.

Although perhaps most interesting today as a point of arrival for
D'Annunzio's novelistic technique as it had been evolving in the ten
years since *Il piacere, Il fuoco* owed much of its early success to its

scandalously detailed (if not always accurate) descriptions of its author's love affair with Duse. When Duse's friends and admirers learned about the book, they were outraged at the sometimes crudely indiscreet treatment they felt she had received in it. But when it was suggested to the actress herself that *Il fuoco* might harm her career and good name, she responded that she "knew the novel and had authorized its printing," judging her own suffering unimportant when it came to "adding another masterpiece to Italian literature. Besides," she went on, "I am forty years old . . . and in love!"[24] Partly because of the scandal it caused, *Il fuoco* found eager readers from the moment it was published: first in Italy, then in France, finally in America where it was lumped among other "nasty Italian novels"[25] currently endangering the morals of susceptible new world readers.

From the start *Il fuoco* was billed as the first volume in a series of three "Novels of the Pomegranate" meant to follow the earlier trilogies of the Rose and of the Lily, with the pomegranate of the title symbolizing the Nietzschean joy that was by now an integral part of D'Annunzio's thinking.[26] But although *La vittoria dell'uomo* (Man's victory) and *Trionfo della vita* (Triumph of life) were supposed to complete the story that *Il fuoco* begins, the two volumes of the sequel (like those of the previous Lily trilogy) were never written.

Since much of *Il fuoco* is concerned with D'Annunzio's ideas about the stage, one reading of this novel is as a kind of fulcrum between his narrative work of the early 1890s and his attempts later in the decade to "awaken souls" through the establishment of an Italian national theater. But even though this theater—planned to rival and eventually surpass Wagner's *Festspieltheater* at Bayreuth—is described at length in *Il fuoco*, it was never realized either in its pages or in the checkered actuality of D'Annunzio's career as a playwright.

Although plot is even less important in *Il fuoco* than it was in *Le vergini delle rocce*, the novel does contain three areas of recurrent narrative interest: the playing out of the asymmetrical love affair between the writer, orator, and musician Stelio Effrena and the actress known as "Perdita" or "la Foscarina"; the celebration of the literary genius and political potential of Effrena as the latest incarnation of the D'Annunzian Superman; and the lush descriptions of Venice and the surrounding mainland in the decline of both the year and the city's artistic and imperial hegemony. Images of old age, decadence, and death crowd the background of this book. They are important, for example, in the story of the Countess Glanegg, whose response to her own aging is to retire into a Venetian palace without mirrors or visitors where she waits for death amid the memory of her past beauty; in the episodes involving the wrinkled but lively Englishwoman and greyhound fancier, Lady Myrta; and in the account of the death and funeral transport of Wagner in 1883 which takes up the novel's last pages. Throughout the book the city of Venice is presented in the sunset of its history, cut off from contemporary life much like Countess Glanegg in her palace, but still aglow with memories of a glorious past. This past, especially the city's artistic and imperialistic accomplishments, is the subject of Stelio Effrena's lengthy oration in its first section, the "Allegory of Autumn," which describes this season's mystical marriage with the city of the lagoons. Although this rhetorical tour de force establishes Effrena's credentials as an exceptional being and wins him the admiration of all who hear him, its metaphorical overdetermination and inflated rhetoric have made it much less attractive to the more diffident readership of the post-Fascist era. The speech is important, however, for its heated exaltation of a sensually described Venetian history demonstrating "the hidden genius of the race, the ascendent capacity of ideals passed on from our ancestors, the sovereign dignity of the spirit, the indestructible power of Beauty, all the lofty values despised by the newest barbarians" (*Romanzi*, 2.625).

One of Stelio's most enthusiastic admirers in this novel is the Duse character, Foscarina, and she too is associated with the theme of old age and death. Even though Duse herself was only five years older than D'Annunzio, Foscarina seems to be significantly older than Stelio, a disparity that both attracts and repels her lover. In her long career of baring intimate levels of her emotional being to the multitudes for whom she has performed, Foscarina has acquired a kind of impurity that Stelio finds immensely attractive. For her lover, even the folds of Foscarina's skirts "bear the collected mute frenzy of those distant multitudes from whose massed animality her cry of passion, wrench of pain, or deathly silence had given rise to the sudden and divine shudder of art" (593). Stelio is attracted to Foscarina not only because she is a practiced lover, but also because she can help him satisfy his artistic ambitions. "In her he no longer saw the lover of one night, her body ripened by protracted ardor and laden with voluptuous knowledge; but the marvelous instrument of a new art, the promulgator of great poetry" (617). For Stelio, Foscarina is an acting tool he can use "to inflame the world with [him]self" (839). Like the Ideal Spouse of *Le vergini delle rocce*, she too is to be a breeder—though the aim of her creative collaboration with the Superman is "Supertheater" rather than a "Superbambino." In this task she must completely submerge her own wishes and personality, content to serve Stelio like "a thing to be clutched in his fist, a ring for his finger, a glove, a piece of clothing, a word to be uttered or not, a wine to be drunk or spilled upon the ground" (702). While Stelio sometimes shows great tenderness to Foscarina, his attitude is tinged with the same sadomasochism that has been remarked before in D'Annunzio's work. For example, in a famous episode in a hedge-maze at Stra in the Venetian hinterland, Stelio hides in the bushes from the increasingly disoriented actress until she is beside herself with terror and frustration and collapses in tears to the ground. But there are kinder, even admiring descriptions of Duse/Foscarina too, such as the moving evocation of her difficult youth as a child struggling with the challenges of poverty and life on the road as well as with the exigencies of her art—pages that in some ways are the most successful in this otherwise highly autocelebratory and stylistically overblown work.

In D'Annunzio's sixth novel what had previously been a desire for personal domination and sexual mastery has become a complex ambition that is sexual, artistic, and political all at once. His new hero is beset by an "insatiable desire for domination, success, and pleasure" (593)— not just for pleasure. In one of the many passages stressing his belief in the identity of aesthetic and political ambition, Stelio insists that a line of poetic drama, a successful political speech, and a weapon wielded on the battlefield are essential equivalents in that they all aim to excite the flashes of beauty that thrill the hearts of Superior Men (660). For Stelio, who in other times might well have been able "to conquer an Archipelago" (728), an artist gripped by creative frenzy is not unlike a warrior besieging a city. Both of these figures are seeking domination, in the case of the artist through an Idea that will "live forever like a dominating force in the midst of mankind" (852). In the theory of aggression put forward in Il fuoco, sexual, aesthetic, and political ambition can all be rallied beneath the banner of "la parola dominatrice"—the "dominating word" that is the hallmark of the Superman.

In D'Annunzio's previous writing the crowd was usually disdained as an antiaesthetic "beast" from which the Superior Individual kept his distance. In Il fuoco, however, Effrena takes pride not only in his ability to dominate the masses but to stir them to action. For Effrena, his attitude here reminiscent of much twentieth-century messianism, "the spoken word, straightforwardly directed at a multitude, should have no other purpose but action, even violent action" (594). This embrace of activism by a hero, who for the first time in a novel by D'Annunzio is both successful and popularly acclaimed, is also a new way to deal with that old bugaboo, reality. Through his forceful utilization of "la parola dominatrice," the Superman is able to sublimate the existential anguish that had bedeviled D'Annunzio's previous heroes in a political activism in which ethical and metaphysical problems can temporarily be set to one side.

In form and stylistic conception *Il fuoco* is the most lyrical and oratorical of all of D'Annunzio's novels. Just as Effrena bewitches the multitudes with the power and beauty of his public orations, so D'Annunzio seems determined to overwhelm and dominate his readers by the force of his style. The highly oratorical tone of *Il fuoco* has not worn well in recent years, at least in some quarters, perhaps because its rhetorical overdetermination has been increasingly associated with repudiated political movements. In its subordination of traditional narrative concerns to a more lyrical approach to novelistic reality, *Il fuoco* is an additional example of D'Annunzio's experimentation with novelistic form and suggestive as well of further lyricizations of the novel in the century that opened with its publication. As for its suggestion that modern politics can best be understood, even practiced, as a branch of theater, this too has become a commonplace in twentieth-century life.

Forse che sì forse che no

D'Annunzio's seventh and last novel, *Forse che sì forse che no* (Maybe yes, maybe no), was not published until 1910, ten years after *Il fuoco*. Much had happened in the intervening decade. During the first years of the twentieth century D'Annunzio continued his writing for the theater begun in the late 1890s. Although the plays he produced were not always well received and for the most part no longer figure in theatrical repertories, the poetry written toward the end of his affair with Duse—especially the summer chronicle of *Alcyone,* most of which was composed during a seaside idyll with her—is among his best and most important work. However, by the time of his new novel, Duse had been replaced in his affections by a procession of other women, among them Alessandra di Rudinì, Giuseppina Mancini, and Natalia de Goloubeff—three exceptional individuals whose often extravagant behavior and neurotic tendencies had a distinct influence on D'Annunzio's depiction of Isabella Inghirami in *Forse che sì forse che no.*

The first decade of the new century was also a time when the debts that D'Annunzio had been accumulating during many years of high life and financial irresponsibility began to be of concern to his creditors as well as to his friends. In 1909 he was compelled to give up his villa, La Capponcina, at Settignano near Florence, and by 1910 his financial situation had become so desperate that he decided, while on a trip to Paris, not to come back to Italy at all; he was to remain in France for the next five years. In addition to his involvement in all of these other matters, shortly before writing *Forse che si forse che no,* D'Annunzio had learned to drive an automobile and had flown for the first time in an airplane—the craft piloted for the occasion by the American Glenn Curtiss.

Forse che si forse che no is one of the best constructed of all D'Annunzio's novels, with a plot that races forward with the dispatch and precision of a finely tuned internal combustion engine. The lexicological delight in precise technological vocabulary its text exhibits, plus its effective natural imagery in the style of *Alcyone,* make the novel one of D'Annunzio's richer prose performances. Much of *Forse che si forse che no*'s plot concerns the love affair between the aviator and sportsman Paolo Tarsis and the passionate and independently minded young widow Isabella Inghirami. As the book opens, Paolo and Isabella are in an open car speeding toward the city of Mantua where they are going to visit the Renaissance palace once the residence of the Gonzaga family. As they race along, Tarsis decides to test Isabella's mettle by accelerating toward an oxcart in the road in front of them and then swerving away from the obstacle at the last minute. Isabella, however, is not intimidated by this maneuver, and the motorists arrive safely in Mantua, where they are joined by Aldo and Vana, Isabella's younger brother and sister. In the course of the visit that they then pay to the Gonzaga palace—a severely neglected monument currently in a state of lamentable disrepair—Paolo kisses Isabella so passionately that he draws blood from her lips. The couple's embrace is noticed by both Vana, who is also in love with Paolo, and Aldo, who is jealous at what has happened for different and more sinister reasons.

After this opening episode the scene shifts to a field near Brescia where Paolo and Giulio Cambiaso, Paolo's longtime friend and companion in exploration and derring-do throughout the world, are preparing for an aviation contest. In the altitude competition that follows, the engine of Giulio's plane malfunctions and he falls to his death. Since in a conversation just before this fatal flight Giulio and Vana had shared a moment of intense spiritual communion, Vana now considers herself Giulio's fiancée and mourns his death bitterly—going so far as to return to the airfield that night in order to join Paolo in the vigil over the dead flyer's corpse.

Book 2 of the novel begins in the Etruscan city of Volterra where Aldo, Vana, and their younger sister Lunella are living in a Renaissance palace that Isabella has inherited from her now-dead husband. Isabella and Paolo, meanwhile, are at the Pisan seashore where they are busy with flights of both an erotic and an aeronautical nature. When the lovers return to Volterra, a violent scene takes place between Isabella and Vana, who even before this had been on the point of killing herself by leaping off the rim of "le Balze," a treacherous cliff on the city's edge. Later, all five of the novel's characters make an excursion to an Etruscan tomb not far from the city. During a moment of accidental darkness while they are inside this structure, Vana kisses Paolo's hand in a desperate attempt to win him over to her, while Aldo, calculating that he will at first be mistaken for Paolo, kisses Isabella on the mouth in a bold declaration of his incestuous desire.

The plot sufficiently thickened by these maneuvers, the scene shifts to Florence. In the novel's concluding section, Vana, who is now beside herself with jealousy, reveals to Paolo that Aldo and Isabella are lovers. When Isabella refuses to deny this, Paolo attacks her physically, blacking her eyes and bruising her arms and body before carrying her off to bed for a final bout of passion. The next morning Paolo and Isabella learn that Vana has committed suicide. Unable to bear the weight of her grief and possible complicity in her sister's death, and after an encounter with equivocal and dangerous company that she meets in the course of some erratic wandering through the city, Isabella loses her mind and is committed to a mental hospital. Paolo, who has had enough of what he calls this "sewer" of passion, incest, cruelty, and death, returns to his airplane for a solo trip across the Tyrrhenian Sea. His flight, which he begins without much thought for where he might be going, does not end—as it seems at first it is going to—with his death at sea, but is concluded instead with a forced landing on a beach in Sardinia. Although Paolo has burned his foot in this incident, his flight has been a victorious one. As he calls on the "spirits of the sea" in the novel's concluding lines to help medicate his wounded member, he is a heroic figure who has successfully shrugged off the terrestial restrictions threatening him.

Although Paolo Tarsis is another example of the D'Annunzian Superman, there are important differences between him and previous exemplars
of the Nietzschean ideal in D'Annunzio's fiction. Not a potential sire
of kings like Claudio Cantelmo, or a successful orator and dominator
of multitudes like Stelio Effrena, Tarsis demonstrates his exceptionality
through displays of physical courage rather than through words. Of
middle-class rather than aristocratic origins, he does not feel out of
place in the modern world whose transportation and communication
devices (this is perhaps the first European novel in which a telephone
call figures importantly in the plot) he dominates as readily and effortlessly
as he does women. Tarsis is not an aesthete, or even an intellectual,
but a sportsman and explorer: a man of action. Although he lives alone
and seems self-sufficient, he is not a lonely exception but enjoys the
company of his friend Giulio and depends as well on the assistance he
receives from the mechanics who help keep both his car and his airplane
running. Disinterested in artistic pursuits and with a preference for male
company rather than the world of women, Paolo is in many ways the
opposite of the handsome and artistically gifted, but passive and corrupt
Aldo, whose negative valuation in this novel suggests a repudiation by
D'Annunzio of the more exclusively aesthetic ideals represented by
similar types in his previous fiction.

Isabella Inghirami, for her part, is one of D'Annunzio's most com-
pelling and powerfully drawn "Superfemmine." In an important scene
after Paolo has accused her of incestuous relations with Aldo, she explains
to her shocked lover that, as far as she is concerned, "love, like all
divine forces, is not really exalted except in a trinity." For Isabella, it
is only in this triangular fashion that love can reach its own platonic
heights. To do so it must "disdain happiness in favor of an unknown
but infinitely higher good, toward which the soul tends continuously,
rapt by the purest of sorrows, the sorrow of desperation" (2.1126).
Isabella is proud of her "divine sense of suffering" and considers herself
a "severe science" of sexual practice. In her frenetic and unrestrained
masochism ("Know me . . . seek me . . . reach me . . . kill me,"
she urges her lover [1137]), she is hoping to achieve not harmony but
a spiritual and physical disequilibrium that will enable her to attain
the understanding she longs for. It is through this radical imbalance
that she hopes to be able to reach what she calls "the bottom of the
abyss, or is it the subterranean temple" (1127).

Much of Isabella's erotic and platonic quest takes place in a meta-
physically suggestive landscape reminiscent of Dante's *Inferno,* to which

there are frequent references in the Volterra section of the book. A creature whose natural habitat is the earth rather than the sea or the air, Isabella seems bound to a world of matriarchy, incest, primitive communism, and the religion of the Great Mother in sharp contrast with Paolo's preferred environment of sea and air, internal combustion machines, heroic individualism, and male camaraderie. Although Paolo and Isabella can achieve a significant combustion of their own while at the seashore or even high in the air in his airplane, they break inevitably apart once she reestablishes contact with her native earth. Heavy with considerations of family, history, prehistory, and culture stretching from the Etruscans to modern times, Volterra is unlike the empty spaces of the Asia or Africa where Paolo has spent much of his life exploring. Like the earth itself, Volterra and Isabella are a drag on Paolo's efforts to be "solitary, free, far from tormenting earth" (924), the ideal condition he is seeking. His struggle is thus with Isabella not only as woman and delimiting sexuality ("Her frail flesh assumed an insurmountable greatness . . . limiting his destiny like a mountain limits a kingdom" [1073]), but also as representative of the society, history, and culture he is trying to transcend. Paolo's flight away from the Italian coast and across the sea, therefore, is a flight into nothingness in both a personal and a cultural sense.

At its conclusion, however, as Roberto Tessari has pointed out in an interpretation of this book that has been followed here, Tarsis has not succeeded in establishing contact with the "reactionary utopia of a society of Homeric companions whose sole scope for action is a confrontation with death."[27] The "spirits of the sea" that soothe his scorched foot on the novel's last page are simply further instances of the primal mother he has been fleeing, an "archetype of the womb, the comforting prenatal condition." In this final scene Paolo's "Dionysian will to tragic self-confirmation is revealed as a fierce mask on the face of a little boy anxious to feel himself a 'god' while clasped in his mother's warm embrace."[28] In his attempt to escape from the world of women and from an earthbound civilization, Tarsis has turned to the male-centered technology of the new industrial nation that Italy was attempting to become in the first years of the twentieth century. The text thus represents a turning away from a politics of nostalgia to a more up-to-date nationalism based on industry and industrial supermen in a new reactionary position of a kind that was beginning to emerge throughout Europe on the eve of World War I.

Chapter Four

The Major Poetry: *Alcyone* and the Other *Laudi*

The *Laudi*

Early in the *Laus vitae* section of D'Annunzio's *Laudi* the hero of this long poem complains that although he has succeeded in daring everything that life has to offer, his human powers have not been able to match his desires:

> Tutto fu ambito
> e tutto fu tentato.
> Ah perchè non è infinito
> come il desiderio, il potere
> umano?
>
> (1.85–89)

[Everything was dared / and everything attempted. / Ah why is human power / not as infinite as desire?]

Only a few lines later, however, D'Annunzio's hero has found a way to overcome the disparity between the infinity of desire and the limits of the human condition. After noting again how "Tutto fu ambito / e tutto fu tentato," he now goes on to say:

> Quel che non fu fatto
> io lo sognai;
> e tanto era l'ardore
> che il sogno eguagliò l'atto.
>
> (1.106–11)

[Everything was dared, / and everything attempted. / That left undone / I dreamed; / and with such ardor / that the dream was the same as the act.]

D'Annunzio's *Laudi* are both the product and the story of boundless ambition reinforced by dreams whenever ability falls short of desire;

66

they are the boldest, the most original, and—in the case of *Alcyone*— the most successful of all this writer's poetic achievements.

Although D'Annunzio planned to write seven volumes of *Laudi* (one for each of the daughters of Atlas transformed into the seven stars of the Pleiades), only four ever saw print: *Maia* in 1903, *Elettra* and *Alcyone* in a single volume of 1904, and *Merope* in 1912. Usually referred to simply as *Laudi* (that is, hymns of praise), the collection's complete title is *Laudi del cielo del mare della terra e degli eroi* (Praises of sky, sea, earth, and heroes). As the long title indicates, in the cosmic system proposed by these poems, earth, air, fire, and water have been transformed into earth, sky, sea, and heroes—with a new race of exceptional humans taking over the function of the destructive and generative element of fire as it appears in traditional cosmologies.

Maia

Although *Maia* was written later than some of the work in *Elettra* and *Alcyone*, this first volume in the series is meant as a prologue to the entire sequence. With the exception of its two prefatory lyrics— "Alle Pleiadi e ai Fati" (To the Pleiades and the Fates) and "L'Annunzio" or "The annunciation" (but with an additional play on the poet's last name)—*Maia* is made up of a single poem: the 8,400 lines of *Laus vitae* (Praise of life), a work that D'Annunzio himself styled a "poema totale" or "total poem," indeed "the only poem of total life after [Dante's] *Comedy*."[1] Much of the first part of this long, allegorical narrative describes a voyage to Greece based on D'Annunzio's own trips to that country in 1895 with Scarfoglio and in 1899 with Duse, though the poet's impressions then have been qualified by consultation of accounts by other travelers and writers on the subject.[2]

Laus vitae's ample proportions, extensive use of repetition and anaphora, and exhaustive catalogs—all in a context of intense autocelebration—may bring Whitman, especially the *Song of Myself*, to mind and D'Annunzio seems to have been acquainted with the American writer's work by the time that he wrote it. The poem could also be compared to Ezra Pound's *Cantos* or Nikos Kazantsakis's *The Odyssey: A Modern Sequel*, two Mediterranean-centered epics that in the case of Pound's *Cantos* also intermittently employs an elevated, "bardic" tone like that used here. Like Pound and Kazantsakis, in *Laus vitae* D'Annunzio juxtaposes his vision of a newly rediscovered and still-vital classical civilization against a degraded modern age and sometimes indulges in references to distant or little-known historical or mythological events that can seem more incantatory than illuminating.

Like D'Annunzio's oratorical novels of the late 1890s, *Laus vitae* contains little in the way of plot or character development but relies instead on its highly ornate and declamatory style to gain the reader's assent to its message. Its story is a heroic one of poetic initiation and discovery. In the first of the two introductory poems *Maia*'s narrator declares that he is a descendant of Dante's Ulysses rather than a follower of the "Galilean" Jesus—a figure he considers too weak for the adventure on which he is embarking. In the second, he announces to the "sons of the earth and of the sea" that "the great God Pan is not dead" but endures as a vital principle in both nature and art. For D'Annunzio in *Laus vitae,* as for Nietzsche before him, ancient Greece is a joyous and life-affirming alternative to an outmoded Christianity whose followers it characterizes as "trembling, bent beneath their accustomed shame," their "foreheads humiliated by the shadow of the cross" (126–130).

Laus vitae begins with an invocation of life—or rather Life—itself. In a single sentence filling all twenty-one lines of its opening stanza, human existence is a "terrible gift of the God" analogous to "a faithful sword, a burning torch, a Gorgon, a Centaur's shirt." As conceived here, life is an almost tangible force that can be brandished like a sword or a torch, and is closely associated with myths of pain and violence like those of the petrifying Medusa or the Centaur Nessus's fatal shirt. As *Laus vitae*'s narrator moves forward on his quest to "pluck the world like an apple," he is fortified by encounters with Dionysius, who gives him a mystic grape cluster, and with Aphrodite, who joins with him in mystical sexual congress. During his journey he learns to listen to the urgings of his own will, pleasure, pride, and instinct: trustworthy emotions that carry him forward like four powerful horses pulling a Roman chariot. His path takes him first through Greece, where he patronizes a Patras brothel that he finds sorely lacking in both hygiene and heroic sensibility, visits Olimpia and Delphos, and takes a purifying dip in the river Alpheus. After a long and beautiful interlude describing the gentle explosion of spring on the hills of Florence, and a subsequent encounter with the Tenth Muse which, appropriately for this poem of poetic and intellectual vitality, is the muse Energy, the scene shifts to Italy.

In the Agro Romano south of Rome the voyager draws additional inspiration from the tough carters and horsemen he meets before moving on to the Sistine Chapel where Michelangelo's heroic frescoes spur him on to his task. In the next section he has retired to the desert where he has a vision of the joyful creation of a "vast prelude to a new song" (19.242–43) celebrating the "mythical force / of a race fertile in labors / and ferocious in arms" (19.389–91). The poet's mission as national bard thus established, *Laus vitae* continues with homage to Carducci as poetic mediator between the glories of ancient Rome and a politically purified Italy where the "Galilean's" grip has been broken forever and the Christian Mater Dolorosa replaced by a sensual and joyful Aphrodite (20.232–45). The poem then concludes with a prayer to Nature and a reiteration of the motto—"Necessario è navigare, / vivere non è necessario" (Seafaring is necessary, living is not)—with which it began.

Although the spatial and temporal itinerary D'Annunzio's hero has followed has taken him mostly through the countrysides of Classical Greece and Renaissance Italy, there have been stops also in the "terrible cities" of the modern world. In these urban environments D'Annunzio's traveler meets a working class brutalized by the imperatives of industrial capitalism and betrayed by both the state and its own demagogic leaders. However, he feels little compassion for these downtrodden masses, which are of interest to him only for the spark of energy that they contain. For D'Annunzio in this poem, social conflicts cannot be resolved by amelioration of the workers' lot but must await a return to those policies of forceful and imaginative domination that made the glorious artistic and political accomplishments of ancient Greece and Renaissance Italy possible.

Politically, *Laus vitae* is elitist, racist, and imperialist. In language from its desert section reminiscent of that later employed by Italy's Axis ally, the enthusiastic poet hails a "new myth" forged from the "holy material / of the race, the deathless / generative substance / of the blood, the pristine / force of the people / turned red hot in the flames before us / like a steely mass / ready to be placed on the anvil" (18.463–70). It is because of the "mythical force" of this race that D'Annunzio dreams of a new *Pax Romana* in which the Mediterranean is once again the *mare nostrum* of imperial Roman memory and Italy has been restored to its rightful place beneath the eyes of the admiring sun.

In terms of style, *Laus vitae*'s long, pulsing cadences make this poem seem just as expansionist in form as it is in ideology. D'Annunzio's belief in the superiority of classical culture has had important consequences for the poem's diction and vocabulary, which follow Greek and Latin linguistic practice to an unusual extent. In *Laus vitae* classicizing

expressions are employed not only in the many episodes dealing with
the monuments and customs of antiquity, but also in the more modern
sequences. An electric tram, for example, is "a cart without axle-tree
/ or yoke, or coursers / shining with blood and foam" that "rushes
untouched along the ground / between the steely pendant rope / and
the twin beckoning steel" (16.14–21). Such use of periphrastic (and
often bombastic) terminology to describe such banal modern objects as
a streetcar tends to drain the poem of historical specificity. In the same
way, D'Annunzio's mythicization of the machine and of the social
conflicts inherent in industrial life diminishes laboring men and women
to uncomprehending acolytes serving a new set of divinities as implacable
and distant from human practice as those of the traditional religion the
poet has set out to discredit. While D'Annunzio's intentions in this
"Praise of Life" may have been to free the spiritually enslaved from
"the Galilean's" life-denying grip, the new ideology he is proposing is
every bit as mortifying and mystifying as the old religion he is combatting.
Furthermore, the freedom and happiness proposed here are not freedom
and happiness for everyone just as the "Dionysian" mythology the work
puts forward is not a tool for liberation but, in the final analysis, an
instrument for class oppression.[3]

Elettra

D'Annunzio published the second and third installments of his *Laudi,*
Elettra and *Alcyone,* in 1903. Although markedly different from each
other in conception and quality, the two collections were first published
in a single volume and only later began to appear separately. *Elettra,*
the second volume in the series, contains a large number of lyrics in
a variety of meters which continue the "praise of heroes" begun in
Maia. The first of its four sections contains odes in praise of Italian
patriots from Dante to the new King Victor Emmanuel III to a grizzled
follower of Garibaldi; the second a description of Garibaldi in retirement
on the island of Caprera; the third praise of Italian and foreign artists
from Giovanni Segantini, Giuseppe Verdi, and Vincenzo Bellini to
Nietzsche and Victor Hugo. The fourth and final section is devoted to
the celebrated "Cities of Silence": fifty-nine verse portraits, mostly in
sonnet form, of Italian cities, plus two concluding songs—one for May
Day, the other the nationalistic "Song of augury for the chosen nation."
    The first poem in *Elettra* is an ode "To the Mountains." In it the
poet calls for a messianic bard to descend from the heights into an

Italy sorely pressed by "arid anxiety" and "atrocious necessities." In an earlier version this work had been titled "To He Who Must Come," the same phrase that appeared in *Le vergini delle rocce* in reference to the future king of Rome. The messianic concerns of this poem are also important in the "Songs of Memory and of Expectation" that begin the "Cities of Silence" section. In them the bard of the opening ode has become a "hero" who "will come from silence, vanquishing death" and whose military rather than aesthetic qualities are what make him heroic.

The "Cities of Silence" section includes some of the most admired and frequently anthologized texts of any that D'Annunzio wrote, among them a beautiful poem on the empty streets of Ferrara and a sonnet on Assisi where the riverbed "is white with the fury of its thirst" and "the olive trees rise like eager flames / from its twisted bank." But in his descriptions of these once-bustling but now silent cities, D'Annunzio is making a political statement as well as composing elegies to past glories. In them he stresses how the brilliant accomplishments of medieval and Renaissance Italy were due to the aggressive and often ruthless actions of a few, highly talented, exceptional individuals. Through their forceful employment of the same intelligence and imagination that gave rise to the extraordinary works of art of the period, these heroic figures created the Renaissance city-states and left their marks on the streets, buildings, and monuments of central and northern Italy that have fallen into such decline since. The desolation currently suffered by the "cities of silence" and the lackluster condition of Italy in general since the Renaissance are due to the absence of the strong-minded leaders who once made Italy the envy of Europe and it is hoped will soon return to take the nation under control.

In the "Canto augurale per la nazione eletta" (Song of augury for the chosen nation) D'Annunzio's political program is made still more explicit. In this concluding poem of *Elettra* a peasant's plow and the prow of a military ship are symbols of Italian efforts in labor and war. The eagle that brushes the plowman's forehead and then comes to rest in a shipyard is an augury of a future launching of the ship destined for "domination of the world" (55). After ten stanzas with the same refrain of "Italia, Italia!," the poem concludes with a vision of the "Latin sea strewn with slaughter" to Italy's greater glory, Italy "flower of all of the races / fragrance of all of the earth, / Italy, Italy / consecrated to the new dawn / with the plow and the prow."

"Seafaring is necessary / Living is not" was the poet's motto both at the beginning and at the end of *Maia*. The concluding poem of *Elettra* makes it clear that the kind of navigation D'Annunzio is proposing is not a voyage of geographical or personal discovery, but an imperialistic foray bent on a racist domination that is justified by the superior artistic and intellectual history of the conquering forces.

Alcyone

In the third installment of D'Annunzio's *Laudi* the stridently political tone of the first two volumes has been considerably attenuated. On the surface at least, *Alcyone*—which only in 1908 began to appear separately from *Elettra*—is the chronicle of a highly successful summer vacation at the Tuscan shore. Its eighty-eight poems in a variety of meters were composed at various intervals between 1899 and 1903, though some of them are based on notebook notations of a much earlier date.[4] In the collection they have been grouped into five loosely coherent narrative sections tracing the passage of one summer in the life of the poet.

In *Alcyone,* as perhaps never before in D'Annunzio's writing, a passion for nomenclature has become a dominant, almost obsessive, consideration. In addition to classicizing locutions like those of *Laus vitae,* and a host of archaisms filched from Dante and other medieval poets, *Alcyone* contains a large number of toponomastic, mythological, botanical, maritime, agricultural, and other unusual or technical terms. D'Annunzio had ferreted out such terminology from such specialized sources as the great Tuscan *Dizionario della lingua italiana* by Niccolò Tommaseo and Bernardo Bellini, Alberto Guglielmotti's *Vocabolario marino e militare,* Egidio Forcellini's *Lexicon* and *Onomasticon totius latinitatis,* and the *Prodromo della flora toscana* by Teodoro Caruel, among others.[5] His cult, as it has been called, of rare and precious vocabulary items in *Alcyone* is not unlike D'Annunzio's attitude toward expensive possessions in *Il piacere* where, as has already been seen, the symbolic overdetermination of certain elements of the novel's decor tends not only to clot the narrative action but also to drain the external world described in the book of historical or affective significance. The specialized vocabulary used in *Alcyone* does not provide D'Annunzio with a more effective instrument for comprehending reality; it reifies and fetishizes poetic language as the single end and purpose of a solipsistic, even onanistic poetic enterprise. At the same time, D'Annunzio's blending of linguistic elements from disparate historical periods and lexical levels into a single glittering metahistorical instrument provides him with an effective tool for the fabrication of mythological realities located outside the usual historical paradigms and subject only to such nonhistorical forces of transformation as the seasonal cycle of change and return that makes up the narrative armature of the volume.

By the time he published *Alcyone* in 1903, D'Annunzio had written almost half his works for the theater and all of his novels except *Forse che si forse che no*. Some of the poetry in the collection was composed while he was still at work on *Il fuoco*, a novel whose artist protagonist shares many traits with the exceptional poet and supreme artificer described in the poetry.[6] *Alcyone* is roughly contemporary as well with *La figlia di Iorio*, a play that also uses intensely stylized language to elevate ordinary lived experience to mythical significance. In addition, it should be remembered that the *Laudi* were D'Annunzio's first poetic compositions after his assimilation of the ideas of Nietzsche.

D'Annunzio himself was very pleased with the book. Writing to Giuseppe Treves in the summer of 1899, he described how the poems in it "were born as spontaneously in my soul as froth on the waves" and noted how in this poetry he had been able to achieve "certain things that [he had] sought in vain for a long time."[7] Published when its author was forty years old, *Alcyone* was an important turning point in D'Annunzio's life and career. After the "tregua" or "pause" that this book brilliantly marks in D'Annunzio's life and art, history began to impinge more insistently and painfully onto the writer's consciousness; partly for this reason, his automythographic writing of later years took a more inward and meditative turn.

If *Laus vitae* was the account of an initiatory quest into the origins of Western culture, and *Elettra* an exortation to greatness inspired by a revisionist pantheon of Italian and European heroes, *Alcyone* describes not the seeking but the possession—tenuously and temporarily, but still the possession—of a truly superior condition of being. In the "Super-poetry" of this volume the task of the exceptional individual is no longer to uncover and revive the mythical past of his race or to move his contemporaries to significant action, but to give voice to the lyrical excitement that he has been privileged to experience during an extraordinary immersion in a highly charged natural setting.[8]

In this most orphic of all his writings D'Annunzio is attempting to respond to the "volontà di dire" (will to speech) that he feels within both him and the things around him. In this volume, as Giorgio Bàrberi Squarotti puts it, "natural objects are a function of the word that the poet gives them, the landscape is as if displaced and disquieted by a desire for speech denied to hills, river, moon, rain, and trees, but granted to the poet who thus resolves the drama of silence imposed on objects and allows them to clarify themselves, to make themselves manifest, to tell how and why they exist and what their deepest secret is."[9] Although the world in *Alcyone* needs the poet if it is to exist at all, the narrator of this volume speaks only at the risk of effacement in the treacherously specular surface of his own fiction. Much of the poignancy of *Alcyone* comes from this sense of the imminent dispersion of both poet and his fictional construct that will take place with the end of summer and of its pages.

The first poem in *Alcyone* is called "La tregua" or "Truce." In it the poet asks permission from the "Despot" of his poetic genius to step away from the world of practicality and reenter "the shadow of the laurel"—that is, return to lyric poetry and a contemplation of nature. In the years since the composition of his last book of lyrics in 1892 D'Annunzio had been busy with such matters as his successful parliamentary campaign, the staging of his first plays, and a tour of readings of his Garibaldian narrative poem, "La notte di Caprera." All these activities had brought him into contact with what he here calls "the fat, opaque Chimera" of his public. After his struggles in the midst of this "vile and heavy human stink," the poet is eager to return to a different kind of environment, a place where "the fauns laugh among the myrtle trees" and "summer burns naked in the midst of the sky"—that is, to a life of the senses and of lyric expression far from his concerns as a public figure.

Alcyone's second poem, "Il fanciullo" (The lad), describes the kind of poetry that D'Annunzio means to create while in contact with this natural world. The flute-playing lad of the title is the offspring of both "the locust and the olive," that is, of Apollo and Athena, poetic technique and wisdom. This child bears within him an orphic force so considerable that he is able to merge into the shapes of the natural world and to dominate such potentially hostile forces as the poisonous snakes that he charms with his music. As such, he is radically different from the "fanciullino" theorized by D'Annunzio's contemporary poet Giovanni Pascoli. Where Pascoli's child stood for an innocent poetic sensibility as yet uncontaminated by literature, D'Annunzio's more knowing youth is a product of both nature and art: entities that the poet now realizes are not contraries but different aspects of the same divine essence. "Natura ed arte," he says in a famous pronouncement, "sono un dio bifronte." "Nature and art are a two-faced god"—a god whose "single heart" the "fanciullo" can hear as it "pulses concealed in his double nature." But even though the mythical stripling has been part of poetry's history since ancient Athens, today "the ancient gods are vanquished" and the "divine statues lie in pieces / toppled from their pedestals." Although the modern poet would like to do appropriate homage to the miraculous creature he has been pursuing, he finds in the end that the flute player and the classical ideals that he represents have evaded his grasp.

The seven remaining poems in the first section of *Alcyone* are concerned with descriptions of natural phenomena, in particular, the arrival of summer on the Tuscan hills near Fiesole. "Lungo l'Affrico nella sera di giugno dopo la pioggia" (Along the Affrico River after the rain on an evening in June) describes the clear sky that stretches above this minor tributary of the Arno and is reflected in the puddles the rain has left behind. As earth and heaven mirror each other, the poet too begins to blend emotionally into the scene he is observing and to share in the land's expectation of divine intervention: "Tutta la terra pare / argilla offerta all'opera d'amore, / un nunzio il grido, e il vespero che muore / un'alba certa" (The entire earth seems / clay proffered to a labor of love / the [swallow's] cry a harbinger, and the dying evening / a certain dawn).

The awaited transfiguration, however, does not take place until the Latin-titled "Furit aestus" (Summer rages—a quote from Virgil's *Aeneid*), the poem which closes this section. In it summer is not a potter's thumb gently molding an expectant world, but a force that arrives with violent images and sharp cries as "L'Ignoto" (the Unknown) asserts its presence in an expectant but frightened world: "L'ora è giunta, o mia Mèsse, l'ora è giunta! / Terribile nel cuore del meriggio / pesa, o Mèsse, la tua maturità." (The hour has arrived, oh my harvest, the hour has come! / Terrible in the heart of noon / Your ripeness, oh harvest, presses down.)

All of *Alcyone*'s first section is set in June, before the arrival of this "terrible" summer. In "La sera fiesolana" (Fiesole evening) the interpenetration of psychological and natural conditions seen in "Lungo l'Affrico" is once again the subject of the poet's revery. In this work the poet and his lady compare the words he whispers to her at evening with the effects of the time of day on the landscape:

Dolci le mie parole ne la sera
ti sien come la pioggia che bruiva
tepida e fuggitiva,
commiato lacrimoso della primavera,
su i gelsi e su gli olmi e su le viti
e su i pini dai novelli rosei diti
che giocano con l'aura che si perde,
e su'l grano che non è biondo ancora
e non è verde,
e su'l fieno che già patì la falce
e trascolora,
e su gli olivi, su i fratelli olivi
che fan di santità pallidi i clivi
e sorridenti.

                                    (18–31)

[Let my words in the evening / be gentle as the rain that rustled / tepid and fleetingly / spring's teary goodbye, / on the mulberry trees, the elms, the grapevines / and on the pines with their new pink fingers / that play with the dying breeze, / and on the wheat that is not yet blond / but is not green, / and on the hay that has endured the sickle / and changes color, / and on the olives, on the brother olives / that render the hillsides / wan and smiling with sanctity].

Most of the compositions in *Alcyone*'s first section share the gentle tones of the poems just examined, though frequently with a hint of violence lingering somewhere in the background (hay that has "endured the sickle" in the lines quoted above; cornflowers and wild poppies mowed down with the wheat in "La spiga" [The ear of wheat]). Poems like "La spiga" and "L'ulivo" (The olive tree), with their biblical or Franciscan cadences (both begin with the phrase "Laudato/a sia" [Let praise be given], which is also the *incipit* of the individual sections of St. Francis of Assisi's well-known *Laudes creaturarum*), seem bent on recapturing a perceptual virginity of the sort associated with St. Francis and his circle or even with Pascoli's "Fanciullino." Throughout this first group of texts the dominant tone has been calm and idyllic, while the imagery—though often mediated by such Renaissance and Pre-Renaissance works as the fourteenth-century anonymous Tuscan translation of Palladius's *De re rustica* and the minor writings of Boccaccio, and by assiduous consultation of the Tommaseo-Bellini dictionary—has been that of the rural countryside near Florence.

But with "Furit aestus" the mood changes sharply. In the dithyramb that follows—one of four such compositions that D'Annunzio uses to mark section beginnings—the scene shifts to a description of "the horses of the sun" and wheat threshing in the Roman *campagna* in July. This long poem marks a return to the language and nationalistic enthusiasms of the earlier volumes of the *Laudi* as Rome is presented as "an incombustible force, / a seedbed of glory, / firstborn daughter from the furrow / of the violent [Romulus]" (42–45). The lyrics that follow, however, are set in Tuscany at the Arno estuary where the poet and his lady, the "Ermione" who is the poetic persona for Eleonora Duse in the volume, are spending a summer holiday. The poems describing their idyll are filled with images of the river, the sea, and the inland mountains of Tuscany in the background; and with the birds, flowers, and plants, and the wild horses of the region. They are filled too with the happiness of the two lovers during a sojourn when, as they exclaim in "Bocca d'Arno" (Mouth of the Arno), "Forse conosceremo noi la piena / felicità dell'onda / libera e delle forti ali dischiuse / e dell'inno selvaggio che si sfrena." [Perhaps we shall come to know the sheer / happiness of the unfettered / wave and of powerful open wings / and of the savage hymn's unleashing.]

In these lyrics setting and sensibility are dissolved into a musicality that is the ultimate sign of the lovers' happiness as well as of D'Annunzio's achievement as a poet. "La pioggia nel pineto" (Rain in the pinegrove)—perhaps the most famous of all his lyric compositions—describes a stroll through a seaside forest transformed by a summer shower into a musical sounding board. As the insistent rhythms reproduce the patter of the rain—first on the trees and bushes, then on the couple's clothing and faces, and finally onto their thoughts and the "fable of love" that holds now one and then the other in its illusory grasp—nature and language emerge from the rhythmic and harmonic texture as if scrubbed clean of all previous use. This freshness, however, is qualified by other considerations, the darker, froggy notes of the "daughter of mud" whose voice is heard in the background; in the same way, the loving communion praised by the poem is explicitly labeled an "illusion" not destined to last. D'Annunzio was aware of the limited duration of the "lyrical moments" that he has captured in *Alcyone*. In "Le stirpi canore" (Melodious offspring)—a celebration of the poet's success at matching his words with such natural phenomena as forests, waves, roots, skies, brambles, smoke, flowers, and dew—the final image is of poetic discourse stretched "tenuous as cobwebs" between the stalks of two trembling plants.

After the delicately beautiful "Innanzi l'alba" (Before dawn) and a number of other poems describing the natural landscape, "Meriggio" (Midday) summarizes the poet's relation to his environment and to the language he uses to dominate this world. As he takes the sun on the beach, the speaker senses that his body is merging into his surroundings as his "supine force" becomes "imprinted on the sand, / and dispersed into the sea." As the transformation continues, "the river is my blood, / the mountain my forehead, / the forests my pubis, / the haze my sweat" until the poet seems to have lost all identity:

> Ardo, riluco
> E non ho più nome.
> E l'alpi e l'isole e i golfi
> e i capi e i fari e i boschi
> e i foci ch'io nomai
> non han più l'usato nome
> che suona in labbra umane.
> Non ho più nome nè sorte
> tra gli uomini; ma il mio nome
> è Meriggio. In tutto io vivo
> tacito come la Morte.
> E la mia vita è divina.
>
> (98–109)

[I burn and glisten. / And no longer have a name. / And the mountains the islands the gulfs / and the capes and the lighthouses and the forests / and the outlets that I named / no longer have the usual names / that sound on human lips. / I have neither name nor fate / among men; but my name / is Midday. I live in everything / silent as Death. / And my life is godlike.]

It is important to notice here that although he is apparently annihilated by the landscape into which he has merged, the poet—who is now subsumed in the names he has given to his world—has attained divine status through an Adamic renaming of the natural world about him. Although he too has been transformed into pure textuality, the text that results is of his own creation, a verbal world into which the poet has written himself as hero and dominant force before disappearing.

The dithyramb that follows tells the story of Glaucus, a fisherman whose transformation into a seagod is mentioned by both Ovid and

Dante. Like the poet in "Meriggio," Glaucus too wants to cast off his present identity and return to the godlike condition he enjoyed beneath the waves but now seems to have lost irrevocably: "O Gods of the deep," he cries at the end of this strange and beautiful poem, "call back the exile / restore his godhead to him!" Many of the other poems in this section, which is set in July at the Tuscan shore, deal with metamorphosis. In "L'oleandro" (Oleander) the tale of Daphne and Apollo is given some twists not found in Ovid, as the maiden—who in D'Annunzio's version would far prefer the embraces of a god to life as a tree—calls out in passionate and desperate reproach to the sun god who has reached her too late:

> Prendimi, strappami alla terra atroce
> che mi si prende e beve il sangue mio!
> Tutto furente m'hai perseguitata
> ed or più non mi vuoi? Me sciagurata!
> Salva mio grembo per lo tuo desìo!
>   (297–301)

[Take me, tear me away from the atrocious earth / that is seizing me and drinking my blood! / Furious in pursuit, / how can you want me no longer? Oh unhappy me! / Preserve my body for your desire!]

In the virtuoso rhythms and language of "L'onda" (Wave) a different sort of transformation is described as the wave changes color, shape, and names before turning first into Ermione, then into the "strofe lunga" or "long stanza" of the describing text. As in "Meriggio," in "L'onda" too the subject of the poetry has become one with the poetic activity itself.

The fourth part of Alcyone opens with "Stabat nuda aestas" (Summer stood naked—the Latin title echoes a verse by Ovid); the dithyramb that follows describes the chase, capture, and physical conquest of Summer as a beautiful woman. But despite this victory, by now the season is beginning to decline, and the poems in the part of the volume set in August are increasingly melancholy. In "Versilia" (the name of the wood nymph in the poem and of a locality on the coast where the poet finds her) the narrator encounters another nonhuman but beautiful woman. Where in "Meriggio" the poet had merged with nature so completely that he seemed to lose his identity, in "Versilia" nature emerges from its usual alterity as the nymph steps out of the tree in which she has been hiding and offers first to make love with the poet, then to guide him to good hunting. The poem includes passages of fresh and biting sensuality as Versilia, whose tongue is "a tender leaf / drenched with sudden desire," tells the "blue-eyed" speaker of these verses that she has emerged from the bark expressly so that he will touch her, and that she knows how to use her moist lips to make "the honey flow in the hearts of men."

But Versilia's somewhat saucy offer to take the poet hunting if he does not care to make love with her is another sign that summer is declining and vacation time almost over. In line with this autumnal theme "La morte del cervo" (Death of the stag) describes the violent and fatal battle of a stag with a centaur in another figuration of the union of the bestial, the human, and the divine. But in the "Madrigali d'estate" (Summer madrigals), which come soon afterwards, the blood and violence of this poem give way to gently descriptive passages and the melancholy realization that summer has almost disappeared. In "La sabbia del tempo" (Sands of time) the sand of the beach that the poet and his lady have trod so happily all summer long is transformed into the dwindling contents of an hourglass. In "Il vento scrive" (The wind writes) the marks the wind makes on the beach are first darkened by the setting sun and then effaced as nature and the summer experiences the couple has enjoyed fade away into erasure. Finally, in "Nella belletta" (In the mud) the odor of putrefaction and decay that has been lurking like a frog's croak at the edge of hearing throughout this volume comes to the foreground in images of rotting vegetation and the gaseous bubbles released by the August swamp's decay.

The final dithyramb deals with Icarus, his love for Pasiphae, and his flight to the sun and defeat just short of the same solar horses described earlier in the sequence. In the last section of the volume the reigning divinity is no longer the virile and powerful Centaur but the goddess Melancholy.[10] Turning away in his imagination from the fading landscape around him, the poet now dreams seven "Dreams of Distant Lands," all of which begin with the word "September" and describe voyages away from the desolate seashore where the poet stands in the flotsam, bereft of his lover and alone once more in the dying season. *Alcyone* ends on a note of emptiness and loss: loss of the summer that now has come to its inevitable conclusion, loss of Ermione who has gone back to her life "beyond the serene rivers, / beyond the green hills / beyond the blue mountains," loss above all of the gods who have abandoned the hills and the sea, creatures of myth that the brittle and erudite images of this poetry could not prevent from finally crumbling.

Even though it too is rife with appropriations from other writers and terms drawn pedantically from specialized lexicons, in *Alcyone* D'Annunzio has succeeded in articulating an original vision of the world in a voice that is unmistakably his own. The Nietzscheanism that he may have partially misunderstood and has undoubtedly distorted as he adapted it for his own purposes in this volume has become thoroughly Italianized or at least Dannunzianized: for good or for ill made part of the Italian linguistic and rhetorical tradition. In much of his previous poetry D'Annunzio seems to have been looking for a subject. With *Alcyone* he has found one, even if in retrospect (his own revisionist retrospect of 1896, for example) the image of the writer-hero put forward in this third volume of the *Laudi* seems at least potentially a part of his worldview as far back as the first *Canto novo*. *Alcyone* was written at a time in D'Annunzio's career when his verbal abilities were at their peak and when the poet himself seems to have been extremely happy, though this happiness probably derived more from his joy at successes with his writing than from significant events in his personal life—in his relations with Duse, for example. Moreover, even if at the end of the initial poem in the volume the "fanciullo" of classical accomplishment seems to have evaded the modern poet's grasp, in *Alcyone* D'Annunzio has succeeded in merging classical studies and contemporary culture, Greek lyricism, Nietzschean anti-Christianity, and the Italian rhetorical tradition. Even the nationalistic insistence in this volume on the culturally vital connection between Greece and Italy and the consequent primacy of both countries for the contemporary imagination is less overt and perhaps for this reason more acceptable than similar assertions in *Maia* and *Elettra*. Finally, while irony is never an important device in any of D'Annunzio's works, the heroic insistence of *Alcyone* is significantly mitigated by the frequent references to the passage of time and the repeated suggestions of dissolution, death, and erasure at the periphery of poetic creation. It is finally this aspect of the book that gives it a sense of pathos absent in D'Annunzio's earlier work where such matters are referred to explicitly but also somewhat automatically in that they too derive from his models rather than are deeply felt the way they seem to be here.

Chapter Five
Taking the Stage: D'Annunzio's Theater

The *Canzoni della Gesta d'oltremare*

The fourth and fifth of the projected seven volumes of D'Annunzio's *Laudi* represent not only a change in subject matter when compared to *Alcyone*, but also a sharp falling off in poetic accomplishment. The *Canzoni della Gesta d'oltremare* (Songs of deeds beyond the seas), issued in 1912 as *Merope*, the fourth volume of the *Laudi del cielo del mare della terra e degli eroi*, and the *Canti della guerra latina* (Songs of the Latin war), which D'Annunzio grouped for a brief time as the fifth volume in the series, are political propaganda of a jingoistic and frequently racist sort.[1]

The ten "songs" in terza rima that make up *Merope* were written while the poet was in France in the five years preceding World War I; the eighteen poems in various forms—including odes, "psalms," "prayers," and two works in French—of the *Canti della guerra latina* appeared after his return and Italy's intervention in the hostilities. Both collections represent a development of political attitudes, especially the notion that Italy should strive to become a naval power able to dominate the Mediterranean, that had been important components of D'Annunzio's writings not only in the recent *Elettra*, but as far back as *L'Armata d'Italia* of 1888 and the *Odi navali* of 1893.

All of the bellicose and xenophobic songs of the *Canzoni della Gesta d'oltremare* were written for publication in the *Corriere della sera*; all but one appeared in the Milanese daily during the final months of 1911 and the first weeks of 1912. They center on Italy's war of conquest in Libya and support its colonialist ambitions in North Africa and elsewhere within the crumbling Ottoman Empire. Though written for the mass audience of a newspaper reading public, the songs of this volume are so crammed with historical and erudite references as to make their comprehension difficult, and from the beginning D'Annunzio found it necessary to include explanatory notes with them—though even thus buoyed, the poems tend to founder in the high seas of excessive toponymic detail and obscure biographical and historical reference.

The *Canti della guerra latina*

The *Canti della guerra latina* are also war poems, though the theater of operations described is that of the Balkans and Western Europe during World War I rather than North Africa during Italy's earlier colonialist incursions. In these later paeans to Italian military might— the individual poems were written and published between 1914 and 1918, though not collected in a volume until 1933—the religious language and biblical rhythms already evident in *Merope* have become even more overt, as have such racist epithets as the reference to Italy's Austrian neighbors as "Filthy Barbarians" ("Per i combattenti" [For the combatants], 97). In their return in a darker vein to the "praise of heroes" begun in *Elettra,* the *Canti della guerra latina* celebrate such contemporary military and patriotic figures as the king and queen of Italy, the commander-in-chief of the Italian army, the brave Italian foot soldier, and the heroic Italian dead. They also contain, in a passage toward the end of "La preghiera di Sernaglia" (The prayer of Sernaglia— the site of a bloody battle between Italian and Austrian troops), the poet's hopes that Italy's costly intervention in the war will result in something more than a "mutilated victory," an expression that was to find great favor among Italians disappointed with the peace negotiations and that would become practically proverbial in the popular press and elsewhere after the war.

Return to Italy

As this brief description of these two volumes indicates, beginning with the years of his French "exile," D'Annunzio had begun to take public positions on a number of political issues. When the poet returned from France in 1915, his first public act was to deliver an oration at Quarto near Genoa in which he urged his native country to intervene in the war on the side of France and the values of Latin civilization. Like many of his speeches, the Quarto oration was delivered in a highly theatrical context and was couched in extremely dramatic terms. It has long been noticed that D'Annunzio's entrance into active political life in 1897, when he was elected to Parliament on a conservative ticket, coincided with the beginning of his writing for the theater. For D'Annunzio, theater and politics, like nature and art, were another "dio bifronte" or two-faced god—complementary expressions of the same creative impulse. Although they were also a means for him to stay afloat financially and were invariably written with at least one eye cocked anxiously at the box office, the more than a dozen plays, stage spectaculars, opera libretti, and sketches for films that D'Annunzio produced between 1898 and 1914 are examples of theater as politics just as his later political activism is an early example of the commonplace twentieth-century phenomenon of politics as theater.

Ideas of a Theater

As early as 1897, in the electoral speech later known as the "Discorso della siepe" (The hedge speech—a reference to the praise in it of the hedges that delimit private property in rural Italy), D'Annunzio had insisted that military, demagogic, and dramatic activity are all heroic performances and thus essentially equivalents. "Within the crowd," he stated, "there is a hidden beauty from which only the poet and the hero can extract thunderbolts. When that beauty makes itself known in a sudden sound exploding from the theater or a public square or the trenches, then a gush of joy swells the heart of the one who has been able to provoke it—whether with a line of poetry, a public speech, or the mark of his sword. Transmitted to the crowd, a poet's word is an action, the equivalent of a heroic deed."[2]

D'Annunzio's notion of the theater as heroic gesture (and of political activity as performance) is articulated in several passages of *Il fuoco*. In this novel it is evident that the writer D'Annunzio considers his principal rival in his work for the theater is not an Italian playwright at all, but the German opera composer and creator of "total theater," Richard Wagner. Even though a number of D'Annunzio's plays were either written expressly for music or had music added to them at a later date, his mature works of this sort are a kind of grand opera without music, compositions in which the highly charged language is a self-sufficient substitute for the music in conventional opera. When there is musical accompaniment to D'Annunzio's plays—a case in point is the Debussy score for *Le Martyre de Saint Sébastien* (The martyrdom of Saint Sebastian)—it is always secondary to the written text.

D'Annunzio's plays can also be seen as an instrument for gratification through the domination of others, in this case a theatrical audience. In a revealing passage in *Il fuoco* Stelio Effrena explains how in the plays he will write in the future he intends to "decapitate the entire Universe" and then display its Medusa-like head to a crowded theater (*Romanzi*, 2.722). This image of the playwright as a new Perseus who, having slain the petrifying monster of the cosmos, displays his trophy to a stunned audience, makes clear the enormous scope and aggressive nature of D'Annunzio's theatrical ambitions. Although one goal of his theatrical writing was to keep this notoriously improvident writer afloat financially, his plays should also be understood as ritualistic displays of the troubling psychological forces that for D'Annunzio constituted the Medusa of "l'Universo intero."

La città morta

The play at issue in the theater discussions in *Il fuoco* was *La città morta*, which D'Annunzio was working on when he was finishing the novel, and the first of his plays in order of composition. Completed in 1896, *La città morta* was first produced in French and in Paris in 1898 as *La Ville morte*.[3] Its action takes place in present-day Greece where a group of Italian archeologists has uncovered the tombs of the Atrides, just as Heinrich Schliemann had actually done a few years earlier. The leader of the archeological expedition is Leonardo, and he is accompanied in Greece by his sister, Bianca Maria, and by their mutual friends, the poet Alessandro and his blind wife Anna. Conflict develops within this quartet when Alessandro and Bianca Maria discover that they are in love. Although Bianca Maria does her best to resist this passion, when Anna becomes aware of Alessandro's and Bianca Maria's feelings, she tries to clear the way for their union by committing suicide. Leonardo, however, is also incestuously in love with his sister and when he learns of Bianca Maria's love for his married friend, he murders her to keep her from Alessandro's arms. At the conclusion of the play Leonardo declares that he has been purified by his act and that no one has ever loved anyone as intensely as he has loved his sister. When Anna returns to the scene at the final curtain and touches Bianca Maria's body, she is suddenly cured of her blindness.

In *La città morta* D'Annunzio does not retell one classical myth but weaves allusions to several stories in and out of his plot. Bianca Maria, for example, seems to be a composite of several Greek heroines, including Cassandra, Antigone, and Iphigenia, and there are allusions throughout the play to works by Sophocles and Euripides as well as to the Atreus cycle by Aeschylus.[4] Although the play may be said to make use of the standard love triangles of the bourgeois theater of its time, its doubling of both the male and the female characters suggests that in it D'Annunzio is struggling with obsessive taboos rooted in atavistic notions of sexual desire and prohibition. Furthermore, although Bianca Maria's death at the end of the play should restore the order that had been disturbed by the transgressive emotions centering on her,[5] there is also the strong suggestion that the exhumation of the bodies of the ancient heroes has been the infraction that has led to the tragedy. The dialectic of prohibition and transgression in *La città morta* is thus a double one, involving on the one hand the conflict between a heroic past and a profaning present, on the other a clash between the social injunctions against incest and adultery that help to organize social relations, and the claim of the exceptional individual to an unfettered existence beyond such restrictions.

Two Dream Plays

Although written for Duse, *La città morta* was first performed by her archrival, the French actress Sarah Bernhardt. To make partial amends for this slight of the extraordinary woman who was not only the playwright's mistress at the time he wrote this play but was to become his financial backer and the principal interpreter of his theater throughout the world, D'Annunzio created another work expressly for her. The *Sogno d'un mattino di primavera* (A spring morning's dream— the allusion to Shakespeare is obvious) was first performed by Duse in Paris in June 1897—that is, about six months earlier than the Paris premiere of *La città morta* but after final arrangements had been made for its production.[6] This one-act "Sogno" or "Dream" was originally conceived as the first in a cycle of four such plays, one for each of the four seasons. As often happened to D'Annunzio's plans for multiple compositions, however, only two of the projected components of this cycle were in fact written, the other being the *Sogno d'un tramonto d'autunno* (An autumn sunset's dream) of 1898.

The setting for the *Sogno d'un mattino di primavera* is a Tuscan villa in a rather vaguely defined present. Although the play is concerned with such violent matters as (to take them in order) adultery, jealousy, murder, and insanity, almost all of the dramatic action has already transpired before the curtain rises. The play itself is concerned with the madness of its principal character, Isabella. Isabella has lost her wits during a terrible episode when her lover, Giuliano, was killed by her jealous husband. Clasped in her dead lover's adulterous embrace, Isabella clung to Giuliano through a long night of horror and despair as his blood ran out of his body drenching hers. In the morning she was insane. In this work too the principal male and female characters are presented in specular pairs: Isabella has a sister, Beatrice, who is in love with Giuliano's brother, Virginio. Virginio, however, like his brother, seems to prefer the mad Isabella to her sane sister, and at the final curtain Beatrice seems to have been deprived of her chance for happiness by the same tragic event that has deprived her sister of her reason and Virginio's brother of his life. In the confrontation between Isabella and Virginio masquerading as Giuliano that Beatrice and Isabella's doctor mount in an attempt to shock the mad woman from her insanity, this replication through specular characters of the central relationship binding this quartet together is especially apparent. Given the work's insistence on blood and madness, cruelty and pleasure, sex and punishment, with suggestions of incest and necrophilia lurking in the background, it is no wonder that the English censor is reported to have found the *Sogno d'un mattino di primavera* "too strong for London,"[7] though the flowery language and dreamlike atmosphere of this text give the work an oddly innocent air.

The primacy of female desire as treated in the *Sogno d'una mattina di primavera* is even more central to its companion piece, the *Sogno d'un tramonto d'autunno*, which was written in 1897, published in 1898, and first performed by Duse in Livorno in 1905. The play, which has an all-female cast, is set on the shores of the Brenta River near Venice and focuses on the jealousy of the Venetian "dogaressa" Gradeniga. At its conclusion, Gradeniga kills her rival, the courtesan Pantèa, by causing a spell to be cast on her "bucentoro" or ceremonial barge. The enchantment causes the boat to burst into flames that consume both Pantèa, and the unnamed young man Gradeniga is in love with but who has left her for the younger courtesan. The theme of the abandonment of an aging woman for a younger rival, and the Venetian setting in the sunset of the year, the city's predominance, and the principal character's life are elements that tie this play to *Il fuoco*. As in the earlier *Sogno d'una mattina di primavera*, which dealt mainly with remembered action, in this work also violent events that are central to the drama's unfolding are not represented on stage but reported instead by witnesses of offstage action. In this work it is up to Gradeniga's retinue of melodiously named handmaidens to observe and then describe such luridly flamboyant events as the dance of the naked Pantèa in sight of a crowd of frenzied boatmen who call out her name, jostle for positions in the river closer to her barge, and finally storm on board and do battle for her body. Even though Pantèa is present in this play only through such descriptions, the resultant portrait of the irresistible courtesan who drives all men mad with passion is an important first example in D'Annunzio's theater of the sexually insistent "Superfemmina" whose personal potency and impatience with any restrictions on her animal appetites make her as dangerous as she is alluring. Pantèa is thus sister to similar characters in D'Annunzio's novels, while her death by fire at the end of this work looks forward to the conflagrations at the end of such later plays as *La figlia di Iorio* of 1904 and *La nave* of 1908.

La Gioconda

D'Annunzio's next two plays, *La Gioconda* and *La gloria,* were both performed by Eleonora Duse's acting company in 1899 and published the same year. *La Gioconda* (the title is the first name of a principal character) is set among artists and bourgeoisie in contemporary Florence. The standard love triangle it presents centers on the sculptor Lucio Settala, who is caught between middle-class conventions, as represented by his wife Silvia, and the demands of his art in the person of his model and creative inspiration, Gioconda Dianti. Although Lucio's passion for Gioconda is a destructive one that has already led him to a suicide attempt, after which he has been nursed back to life by his faithful wife, in the end he not unexpectedly chooses art and uncertainty over goodness and security. Lucio makes this decision even though Silvia—in a bizarre reprise of an incident from the early "L'eroe"—has further sacrificed herself by allowing her hands to be crushed in order to save a statue by her husband that has toppled over during an altercation. Although Lucio is meant to represent the artist as Superman (his studio is said to be located in a region "beyond good and evil"), he is much weaker than either of the two women in the drama, in this similar to the many other male characters in D'Annunzio's plays who find themselves in thrall to strong-minded and sexy women.

La gloria

Although Silvia sacrifices her hands for the sake of her husband's art[8] and in so doing fits into the role of victimized wife that was conventional in much European drama of this period, Elena Comnèna of *La gloria* (Glory) is not at all inclined to sacrifice for the sake of her men. Another example of the "Superfemmina" previously seen in such characters as Gradeniga and Pantèa, la Comnèna stands at one pole of the opposition between bourgeois values and politics just as Gioconda Dianti had stood at a similar pole in the opposition between bourgeois values and art.

La gloria is the story of the unwilling transfer of political power from one demagogic leader, Cesare Bronte—said to have been modeled on the contemporary politician and statesman Francesco Crispi—to another, Ruggero Flamma—who shares certain traits with Crispi's rival, Felice Cavallotti. But quite apart from its interest as a *pièce-à-clef* representative of certain political attitudes of the day, *La gloria* is important for its insistence that the driving force behind political ambition is a passion for domination that is analogous to and often coexistent with sexual desire. The ruthlessness and unyielding egotism that characterize the "Superfemmina" Elena Comnèna in this play make her both a powerful instigator for political action and an irresistibly desirable sexual partner.

In recent times *La gloria* has also been read as an unwitting prophecy of later events in Italian politics, especially as those politics were played out in the public arena.[9] Like the later, better-known historical Duce of Italy who may or may not have read this play by D'Annunzio, Ruggero Flamma is a brilliantly effective orator able at will to dominate a crowd he nonetheless despises. Since Flamma also relies on street violence as a way of advancing his revolutionary program, and spends hours toiling at night in a room very much like that later occupied by the apparently (and ostentatiously) indefatigable Mussolini, it is evident why so many have found him a bizarre fictional forerunner of the leader of the Fascist regime. There is even a slogan in the play, "Chi si arresta è perduto" (Whoever stops is lost), that was later taken up by Flamma's historical counterpart. Despite such supposedly prophetic elements in this first explicitly political play by D'Annunzio, its use of the expressive modalities and language of the realistic theater of the day for the articulation of these themes of sexual and political domination represented a direction that D'Annunzio was not to follow in his more successful work for the theater.

Francesca da Rimini

Francesca da Rimini of 1902, which was again written with Duse in mind for the title role, marks a revolution in the development of D'Annunzio's stagecraft and attitude to the theater as spectacle. Gone in this work are the conventional situations and language of most of D'Annunzio's theatrical writing to this point. A self-styled "poem of blood and lust," *Francesca da Rimini* (the title is the proper name of a famous character in Dante's *Inferno*) is D'Annunzio's first play in verse and his first play set firmly in the past. It is also his first work to make use of a large number not only of actors and actresses, but also of dancers, musicians, and other nonspeaking participants, and his first work (apart from the two "Sogni") to move away from the standard drawing-room setting to a new kind of spectacular production with elaborate sets, costumes, music, and special effects. *Francesca da Rimini* was later made into an opera with abbreviated book by Tito Ricordi and music by Riccardo Zandonai; the musical version was first performed on 19 February 1914, and has been revived on several occasions since.

The story of *Francesca da Rimini* comes from a celebrated episode in canto 5 of Dante's *Inferno,* supplemented by the legends and chronicles that Dante himself used and the commentary on his text that grew up afterwards. The play takes place in the belligerent and half-savage city-states of northeastern Italy in the early thirteenth century. As the curtain opens, Francesca da Polenta is about to be tricked into marrying the "sciancato" or lame Gianciotto Malatesta of Rimini, who she has been led to believe is his younger, sounder, and much handsomer brother Paolo. During a battle between Guelphs and Ghibellines in Rimini after Gianciotto and Francesca have been married, Francesca and her new brother-in-law realize that they are irremediably in love. Soon afterwards, in a scene based closely on the *Inferno* episode, they make love in Francesca's chambers after reading a suggestive passage from the Lancelot-Guinevere legend. Meanwhile, Malatestino, the youngest and most ferociously impulsive of the Malatesta brothers, has also become attracted to Francesca. When she spurns his crude advances, the furious youth denounces the lovers to Gianciotto. In the play's final scene Francesca's husband returns suddenly from a feigned trip, surprises the adulterous pair in Francesca's bedroom, and kills them both.

In this "poem of blood and lust" D'Annunzio has broken with the conventions of bourgeois drawing-room drama still evident in such earlier plays as *La città morta, La Gioconda,* and *La gloria.* With *Francesca da Rimini,* as Giorgio Bàrberi Squarotti has noted, D'Annunzio seems to have become aware of the difficulty, if not the impossibility, of representing tragic heroism in a world of middle-class norms. Through the almost pedantic re-creation in this costume play of an earlier world of savagery and magnificence, poetry and violent passion, he is able to create what Bàrberi Squarotti calls a protected space for his theatrical discourse in which he can demonstrate "the absolute difference and distance of this theme from bourgeois norms, and thus . . . make evident the exorbitant nature and transgressive character of real tragedy."[10]

However, D'Annunzio seems to have been so carried away by his enthusiasm for the medieval setting for his drama that the result—especially when one considers the highly artificial, archaic, and archliterary language declaimed by the characters in this play—has been condemned by many as little more than literary bric-a-brac. Such criticism points up how much the real protagonist of this play is the deliberately archaic and immensely rich (though also undoubtedly "fake antique") language that D'Annunzio deploys in it.[11]

La figlia di Iorio

La figlia di Iorio (*The Daughter of Jorio,* 1907) belongs to the same season of creative fertility as *Alcyone* and was composed during the same period as many of the poems in that volume. First performed in March 1904 with Irma Gramatica and not Duse in the title role, it was published later that same year. The play is without question D'Annunzio's most frequently performed and successful composition for the theater. Two operas, one by Alberto Franchetti and another by Ildebrando Pizzetti, have been based on it.

Set "many years ago in the land of the Abruzzi," *La figlia di Iorio* is the story of Aligi, a young shepherd whose artistic inclinations and dreamy temperament have placed him at the margins of the archaic peasant society into which he was born. When Mila di Codra, the outcast daughter of Iorio of the title, seeks refuge from a mob of drunken, sun-crazed reapers bent on sexually assaulting her, Aligi gives her sanctuary at the family hearth even though in doing so he risks contaminating his own marriage ceremony, a complex rite that is described in some detail in the play. Aligi's lack of solidarity with the other men and his apparent disregard for their customs are a transgression of the patriarchal code and he is forced to leave the village. In act 2 Aligi and Mila are living in a cave in the hills where they cohabit chastely in the company of such colorful figures of local folklore as a herbalist, a *cavatesori* (treasure-seeker), and a *santo* (rustic saint). Although Aligi is planning to go to Rome with Mila to seek forgiveness from the Pope for his disobedience and ask for a dissolution of his unconsummated

marriage, these plans are spoiled when his father, Lazaro, arrives at the
cave. When Lazaro orders Aligi to stand aside and let him have his
way with Mila, a struggle ensues in which Aligi picks up the axe he
has been using to sculpt the statue of the angel who appeared to him
when Mila sought refuge from the mob, and slays his father with it.

Act 3 takes place back in the village with Aligi about to be executed
as a parricide by having his hand severed and being thrown into the
river in a sack with a vicious mastiff. He is saved, however, when Mila
suddenly claims that she has bewitched the innocent shepherd and then
killed his father. At the final curtain, the daughter of Iorio leaps into
a funeral pyre exclaiming, "La fiamma è bella! La fiamma è bella!"
(The flame is beautiful).

La figlia di Iorio is perhaps D'Annunzio's fullest treatment of the
oedipal themes that have been lurking in the background of several of
his works, from the *Trionfo della morte* of ten years earlier to the
memorialistic writing of the last part of his life. Aligi, the outsider,
artist, and transgressor of conventional codes, is also similar to the other
exceptional individuals who have appeared elsewhere in D'Annunzio's
writing. Mila, though she makes amends at the end of the play for
what are once again male transgressions, and is thus another representative
of the familiar victim figure, also has something of the "Superfemmina"
about her in her stubborn resistance to the pressures of a hidebound
society and her defiant election of a "beautiful" and heroic death. The
entire play, as Pietro Gibellini has pointed out, makes use of a "savage
and archaic world . . . as the amphitheater for such mythical-archetypal
conflicts as those between father and son, shepherd and peasant, conscience
and law, infraction and rite, outsider and tribe."[12] Like *Francesca da
Rimini, La figlia di Iorio* is in verse, but the impossibly archaic and
poetic language—much of which represents a conflation of archaic Tuscan
and Abruzzi usage—makes it a further example of D'Annunzio's
inveterate antirealism. Although the middle-class audiences who cheered
the play in D'Annunzio's own time seem to have been taken in by
his antirealistic and ahistorical representation as corresponding to their
own fantasies of the archaic splendor of peasant life, critics since have
been more severe. The play is often cited today as an example of the
deliberate falsification of the realities of Italian agricultural and provincial
life just as *Francesca da Rimini* is considered a deliberate falsification
of Italian medieval history. Although these strictures are certainly well-
taken, that *La figlia di Iorio* continues to be performed today suggests
that despite its unrealistic treatment of its themes and its melodious

but "fake peasant" dialogue, the play can still stir certain psychomythical realities important to contemporary life.

La fiaccola sotto il moggio

Despite what seemed to be the promising new direction established by *Francesca da Rimini* and *La figlia di Iorio,* in his next two plays D'Annunzio returned to a contemporary setting and the conventions of realist drama. *La fiaccola sotto il moggio* (The light under the bushel, 1905) is set in the Abruzzi, but in a crumbling palace inhabited by a decaying aristocratic family rather than outdoors among agricultural workers. Although the play is in verse, its language is the ordinary discourse of everyday life rather than the mannered but highly poetic idiom of *La figlia di Iorio.* Like its immediate predecessor, *La fiaccola sotto il moggio* is a story of powerful passion within a family, in this case the hatred of a daughter, Gigliola de Sangro, for a stepmother, the ex-servant Angizia, who is now ruling the household where she once served. When Gigliola learns that Angizia has not only married her father, Tibaldo de Sangro, but also killed her mother, she decides to erase this shame from the family honor by murdering the usurping woman. At the last minute, however, Tibaldo kills Angizia instead. In so doing, he not only deprives his daughter of the vengeance she thinks is rightly hers, but also renders Gigliola's own death absurd. For Gigliola, before going on to kill Angizia, has made certain of her own subsequent demise by plunging her arm into a sack of poisonous serpents. The final death of this "Superfemmina" is thus ridiculous and wasteful rather than the heroic gesture that Gigliola had intended.

In *La fiaccola sotto il moggio* D'Annunzio is attempting to insert elements from Greek tragedy (in this case he seems to have been especially influenced by Sophocles' *Electra*) into an everyday context. The play also features a clash between two "Superfemmina" characters, Gigliola and Angizia, who are balanced in it by a pair of weak males: the highly manipulable Tibaldo, who is bitterly aware of his insufficiencies when compared to the doughty ancestors who once occupied the palace where he is now playing out his sordid existence, and Gigliola's spineless brother Simonetto, an Orestes-like figure incapable of the forceful action necessary to resolve the family crisis. Although *La fiaccola sotto il moggio* is one of the more frequently produced of D'Annunzio's plays, the critic Caraccio is surely correct when he says that the work lacks "élan."[13] D'Annunzio's attempt in it to raise his characters to the heroic dimensions necessary for tragedy is a failure because of the incompatability of its tragic themes with its unheroic, naturalistic setting of degradation and decline.

Più che l'amore

Più che l'amore (More than love) of 1906 is the second explicitly political play (the first being La gloria) written by D'Annunzio. Perhaps the biggest flop of all his work for the theater, the composition was soon fitted out with an introduction defending its "unusual daring in interpreting the myth of Prometheus: the necessity for a crime that weighs on the man who has decided to raise himself to the condition of a titan" (xlvi). After this evocation of Prometheus as modified by Nietzsche with a nod to Dostoyevski, the preface goes on to remind D'Annunzio's Italian audience of their "vocation beyond the seas . . . the thirst for adventures and discoveries, the joy of propagating the splendor of the fatherland beyond known frontiers, and the pride in impressing a Latin footstep on an inhospitable soil" (xlvi). As can be seen, thematically Più che l'amore is a blend of several of D'Annunzio's preoccupations in the years just after the turn of the century, especially the doctrine of the Superman for whom all is permitted, and his enthusiastic support of Italian imperialism.[14]

Più che l'amore centers on Corrado Brando, a determined and unconventional middle-class intellectual and explorer whose desire to return to Africa is the passion that means "more than love" to him. Short of the necessary funds to finance such a trip and impeded by the embarrassing fact that he has not only seduced but also impregnated his fiancée, Maria Vesta, Brando solves the first problem by murdering a gambling companion and stealing his winnings, and brushes off the second as not a significant impediment to the accomplishment of his destiny. Brando's plan misfires, however, when he leaves incriminating evidence at the scene of the crime. At the final curtain this latest incarnation of the exceptional being and his faithful Sardinian retainer Rudu are loading the hunting rifles they have brought from Africa in preparation for a battle to the death with the police.

Even though Corrado's best friend, the engineer Virginio Vesta, asserts bravely in the play that "when an entire new generation aspires toward a new Ideal, it is a sign that the great exemplars are about to reappear from the depths of the race" (31), Brando does not seem much in the way of a "great exemplar." Although his killing of the gambler and moneylender Paolo Sutri was obviously influenced by Dostoyevski's *Crime and Punishment* (1867), D'Annunzio's hero is no Raskolnikov. When compared to the soul-searching that wracks Dostoevski's philosophical and ultimately repentant murderer, Brando's heroic gesturing seems shabby, egocentric, and ill-conceived, his crime the result of nothing more exalted than simple greed, and his seduction and abandonment of Maria Vesta an act of callow insensitivity rather than of tragic desperation; Federico Roncoroni is probably right in judging him "ignoble."[15] Although not without certain D'Annunzian fillips, the prose of this play is that of the standard drawing-room comedy. So too, at bottom, are the situations it presents of the abandoned woman who is ready out of "more than love" for her man to sacrifice everything for him, the brave engineer whose technological expertise is a way for him too to "conquer the world," and the circle of loyal friends deeply concerned with the future of their country's cultural heritage who also appear in the course of the action.

La nave

D'Annunzio's next three plays, *La nave* (The ship) of 1908, *Fedra* (Phaedra) of 1909, and *Le Martyre de Saint Sébastien* (The martyrdom of Saint Sebastian) of 1911, represent the culmination of his theatrical writing. While perhaps not his most admired work in this genre, these plays are the most spectacularly and characteristically D'Annunzian— that is to say, transgressive and outrageous—of all that he produced for the theater. As such they would seem to represent the point of arrival at which his labors in this genre had been aiming from the beginning.

La nave was first produced in 1908 for a Roman audience that included the king and queen of Italy. The sumptuous and elaborate sets employed on that occasion were greeted with applause when the curtain rose (the first time, apparently, that such a thing had happened in Italy), and at the termination of the spectacle the royal couple invited the author to their box to compliment him on the play's success.[16] Written in hendecasyllables, *La nave* is set in sixth-century Venice at the time of that city's struggle with the Byzantine Empire for control of the eastern Mediterranean. Its plot once again drips with jealousy, lust, and political ambition, and the heroine and protagonist of the play, Basiliola, is perhaps the most extravagantly "Superfemmina" (and

outrageously proto-camp) of all D'Annunzio's female creations for the
stage.

During the first years of the republic, power in Venice is equally
divided between church and state, institutions headed by two brothers,
Marco and Sergio Gràtico. Basiliola Faledro is the leader of a rival
faction and her own brothers, who appear on stage in a scene that
blends the horrific and the pathetic, have had their eyes and their
tongues torn out by the Gràtico forces. In revenge for this, Basiliola
manages to get both Gràtico brothers to fall in love with her and then
incites them to a public duel in which Marco kills Sergio as the drunken
populace cheers him on. Horrified at what he has done, Marco decides
to launch the warship of the play's title and sail away to the distant
shores of the Adriatic, there to engage in heroic deeds that will serve
to expiate his sin and augment Venetian glory. His eyes now opened
to Basiliola's perfidy, Marco has her seized and is about to nail her to
the prow of the ship as a living figurehead when she breaks free and
flings herself defiantly into the flames that burn on an altar in front
of Saint Mark's cathedral.

Among the concerns in *La nave* that will also be important in
D'Annunzio's next two plays are its description of a clash between
opposing religious customs; a sexually valorized protagonist who defies
any conventions that threaten to prevent the satisfaction of her desires;
the final apotheosis of this protagonist; and a depiction of the past as
a cruel but less inhibited and therefore more vital and authentic time
than our own. Almost all of the dialogue in the play is meant to be
declaimed, much of it to be shouted. Exceptionally oratorical throughout,
the language has been drawn from such specialized sources as the
Guglielmotti dictionary of military and nautical terminology that also
served D'Annunzio in his writing of *Alcyone,* and often seems about
to dissolve into the pure musicality of verbal incantation rather than
to be aimed at theatrical communication of the usual sort. *La nave*
requires elaborate sets and a large cast of characters including several
choruses: of boatbuilders, sailors, prisoners, and competing religious
factions, all of whom chant their parts the way choruses in Verdi or
Wagner sing theirs. The work also contains a number of shocking or
otherwise sensational scenes. These include Basiolola's striptease and
naked dance before the entranced Gràtico and Venetian populace; her
slaughter with bow and arrow of prisoners trapped in the pit of the
Fossa Fuia (when the last remaining of these begs for a kiss, she licks
the arrow's tip before driving it into his chest); and the final bursting

into flames of her long hair as she leaps into the altar fire. In at least the deleterious sense of the term, *La nave* is among the most operatic of all of D'Annunzio's work for the theater.

Fedra

As its title indicates, *Fedra* (the Italian form of Phaedra) is a retelling of the same mythical story that also provided material for important tragedies by Euripides, Seneca, and Racine. D'Annunzio's version of the Phaedra/Hippolytus story was first performed in December 1908 and published the following year; both Ildebrando Pizzetti and Arthur Honneger later wrote music for it. Its principal female character is another version of the "Superfemmina." If not an atheist, Fedra is at least determined to measure her mettle against that of the gods. This is evident from a scene early in the play when she listens entranced to a messenger's story of Capaneus's famous defiance of the divinities during the war against Thebes. Later, when Theseus's son Ippolito is presented with a slave girl seized in that war, Fedra is jealous of the girl's beauty and kills her with her own hand. Then, when Ippolito returns from the hunt and falls asleep on the ground in front of her, Fedra—in this strikingly unlike her more restrained counterparts in Euripides and Seneca—kisses her stepson passionately on the mouth and reveals to him that she is "sick, sleepless, and desperate" (*Tragedie,* 2.329) for his love. When the horrified Ippolito rejects her advances, Fedra first dares him to kill her with a battle-axe ("Hit me! Split me with all your force / down to the waist, so that I / can show you my naked heart, / my smoking heart, burnt for you" [337]), then accuses him to Theseus of having violated her. Cursing his son, Theseus calls on the sea god Poseidon for vengeance. In response to the wrath of Poseidon, tamer of horses, Ippolito is thrown from his horse and has his belly torn open by the animal's teeth. Although the object of her desire is now dead, Fedra is convinced that Ippolito is still hers; at the end of the play she cries defiantly to Artemis that she has successfully subverted the "ancient laws" of that divinity's religion and replaced them with a "secret law" of her own. As the curtain falls Fedra the "Superfemmina" proclaims: "Again I win! / Ippolito, I am with you. At the entrance to night, / oh stars, Fedra the unforgettable, / is smiling at you" (380).

At the end of D'Annunzio's retelling of the Phaedra story, order is not reconfirmed the way it is in a Greek tragedy like that of Euripides.

In D'Annunzio's version the dominant ethical and metaphysical system has been called into question by a powerful woman who chooses death and the underworld rather than renounce her passion. Even though she is finally brought down by Artemis's avenging arrow, Fedra has chosen a "beautiful death" that reconfirms her identity as a creature of dark but splendid passions which, however unacceptable to the present ethical hegemony, nonetheless define her heroic character.

Plays in French

During the time he lived in France, D'Annunzio wrote a number of plays and other works in the language of that country. One of them, *Le Martyre de Saint Sébastien,* deserves to stand (or perhaps fall) right along with *La nave* and *Fedra. Le Martyre de Saint Sébastien* was first performed at the Chatelet in Paris in 1911 and published the same year. It is dedicated to Maurice Barrès and has accompanying music by Claude Debussy. The original production was directed by Michel Fokine with sets and costumes by Léon Bakst and Ida Rubinstein in the title role. Like *La nave,* this play too requires elaborate sets and costumes and has a large number of nonspeaking roles (a production in Lyons in 1952 featured over 600 roles and 400 different costumes; the playbill for the original production speaks of 150 "artistes," 350 "exécutants" and 500 costumes).[17] Just before the première the play was denounced by the Archbishop of Paris (possibly because the male Christian saint was played by a female Jewish dancer) who urged the faithful not to attend. Despite this publicity, the play was not a hit with the Parisian public; it has been revived only sporadically since.

Le Martyre de Saint Sébastien is D'Annunzio's only work for the theater set in classical Rome rather than Greece or Italy. A "mystère" or mystery play rather than a tragedy, it is similar to *Fedra* and *La nave* in that it describes the clash of two rival religions. In this case these are the state religion of Rome and the new Christian cult, where *La nave* depicted the confrontation between a loosely defined rural animism and a nascent Christianity, *Fedra* that of an ancient chthonic cult with the newer Olympian beliefs. As *Le Martyre de Saint Sébastien* opens, the crypto-Christian twins Marco and Marcellino are being threatened with death unless they abjure their faith. But Sébastien, the captain of the emperor's archers who have been guarding the boys, intervenes in their interrogation to declare that he too is a follower of

Christ. After various struggles in which the priests and magicians of the old religion are vanquished by the power of Sébastien's beliefs, the future saint is sentenced to execution by his own archers. Although the bowmen are extremely reluctant to turn on their leader in this way, Sébastien pleads with them to follow the emperor's command and kill him. Pierced by their arrows of love and despair, he dies in an ecstasy that is part religious and part sadomasochistic, and is immediately assumed into heaven.

Although D'Annunzio deals in this play with what are for him the somewhat unusual emotions of religious faith, innocence, and sacrifice, the quite different feelings of lust, jealousy, and fear of the outsider that are so important in his other plays do not fail to make their appearance here as well. The mixture of the sacred and the profane can be seen clearly in the figure of the androgynous protagonist (there is a story that D'Annunzio was inspired to write the play after a close-up inspection of Mme Rubinstein's legs) who is part saint and part Superman, both suffering Christ and overwhelmingly beautiful Adonis. What makes the play unusual in D'Annunzio's canon is its use of the French language. In his later years D'Annunzio admitted that while he had long been able to write in French "rapidement comme en mon langage natal," at the same time he noticed "les déformations de l'esprit et de la sensibilité par ce langage étranger."[18] Whatever these "deformations of spirit and sensibility" might have meant for the Italian author, later critics of this work have judged its French impossibly "macaronic" and the work of a "grand dilettante."[19]

Unfazed, however, by such criticism of his French, some of which began with the play's first reviews, D'Annunzio went on to write two more plays in this language. *La Pisanelle ou la mort parfumée* (Pisanella or perfumed death) of 1913 is an attempted return to many of the themes and modalities of *Le Martyre de Saint Sébastien;* it was again performed with Rubinstein, Bakst, and the Ballets Russes. Perhaps all that needs to be said about this play (and it is said in its subtitle) is that its principal character is smothered by roses at the final curtain. D'Annunzio's other French play is *Le Chèvrefeuille* (Honeysuckle) which was performed in Paris in 1913 and in Italian as *Il ferro* (The weapon) in Turin, Rome, and Milan the year after. A pallid reprise of the characters and situations of *La fiaccola sotto il moggio,* this play too indicates that by this time in his life D'Annunzio was turning his thoughts to other matters.

Other Theatrical Ventures

Before considering these other matters, it should be mentioned that during this same period just before the beginning of the war, D'Annunzio also produced a number of minor works for the theater. The first of these was a libretto, *La Parisina* (the proper name of its female protagonist) for an opera by Mascagni. The theme for this work comes from the same material that was utilized in *Francesca da Rimini,* and *La Parisina* was billed as the second work in the Malatesta cycle. It had its premiere in 1913 and was also performed without music in 1921. In 1914 D'Annunzio wrote the captions for what turned out to be an extremely successful silent film by Giovanni Pastrone, *Cabiria,* a kind of prototype for Hollywood's later biblical blockbusters, complete with bare-chested hero and squadrons of slave girls. Finally D'Annunzio also began a libretto on *La crociata degli innocenti* (The children's crusade), which was intended for music by Giacomo Puccini but never completed.

Although D'Annunzio's plays have never received the same critical attention as his novels and poetry, his work in this area deserves consideration by anyone who wishes to understand this writer's attitude to the relationships between author and public, action and writing, domination and subservience. His work for the theater was always aimed at something beyond the confines of the stage. Even though too many of his tragedies read (and act) like the last scenes of compositions where all the action was in the earlier acts, and his writing for the stage tends more toward the sensational than the reflective, D'Annunzio's is a theater of action in the sense that his plays were meant to move his audiences to significant activity after they had left the theater. Personal psycho-dramas in which he did not hesitate (in that still pre-Freudian age in which his plays appeared) to lay out even the darkest of his personal obsessions for the inspection of all who cared to consider them, D'Annunzio's plays were at the same time essential elements in his self-appointed mission as national mythographer and thus as creator of a new politics and a new unconscious for Italy.

Chapter Six

Ariel Armed: From Pen to Sword to Pen

The Soldier Poet

If D'Annunzio's writing for the theater in the first years of the new century had important political overtones, his political activities during and after Italy's entry into World War I took on many of the characteristics of a carefully staged theatrical spectacle. D'Annunzio's political and military adventures in this period were the most flamboyant and successful of all of his artistic creations—at least for the mass audience in Italy that did not attend the theater or read novels or poetry, but did follow newspaper accounts of this writer's exploits. Much of the fame that he achieved during the later years of his life— and the subsequent critical reaction to his work even many years afterward—were the result of his political activism of this period. In *L'Armata d'Italia* of 1888 D'Annunzio had said that he wanted to be something more than a "mere poet." Beginning with World War I, this goal was achieved. From that point on, it was Mussolini, the political demagogue, rather than Carducci, the poet of the Third Italy, who became his principal rival for the attention of his contemporaries and a possible place in history.

The World War, Fiume, and Fascism

When World War I broke out in July 1914, D'Annunzio was living in France, and Italy was not yet a participant in the hostilities. When Italy did join the war (despite appearances, the decision to do so had been made before D'Annunzio's Quarto speech), D'Annunzio quickly had himself mustered back into armed service.[1] Even though fifty-two years old at the time, the "warrior poet" ended up serving in the Italian infantry, air force, and navy, and surprised his critics by doing so with undeniable bravery. Already familiar with airplanes from the days of *Forse che sì forse che no,* he flew as passenger and sometime

bombardier on a number of missions behind enemy lines, during one
of which, the celebrated "Flight over Vienna," he dropped red, white,
and green leaflets onto the Austrian capital inviting its citizens to throw
down their arms and surrender. Leaflets were left behind too after the
"Beffa di Buccari" (The mocking at Buccari), a torpedo-boat excursion
into a Dalmatian harbor that resulted in the sinking of an Austrian
ship. Such exploits attracted a good deal of attention in Italy and
elsewhere: partly because of the cachet D'Annunzio already enjoyed,
partly because his were highly visible acts of individual heroism in what
was otherwise a bleak war of attrition waged by masses of largely
anonymous troops.[2]

But the most famous of D'Annunzio's military adventures took place
after the war was over. In September 1919 with hostilities at an end
but the status of some of the territories that had belonged to the
contending powers still uncertain, D'Annunzio led a group of legionnaires
south from Trieste into the city of Fiume on the Istrian coast of what
is today Yugoslavia. This group of patriots, dissidents, and adventurers
seized the city, declared it Italian, and proclaimed D'Annunzio its new
governor. To his own delight, the dismay of the Italian government,
and the astonishment of the world, D'Annunzio remained in possession
of this middle-sized Adriatic port for sixteen months, a modern-day
Sancho Panza governing his island—though without the blessing of his
superiors that Cervantes's fictional character enjoyed. In Fiume, D'Annunzio coauthored a utopian and libertarian constitution for the new
state, made frequent speeches to the masses assembled beneath his
balcony, and did his best to translate his literary ideals into political
reality. In the process he invented much of what later became the
mottoes and rituals of Italian Fascism, although when the March on
Rome and coup d'état took place in 1922, it was not D'Annunzio the
Comandante but Mussolini the Duce who emerged as the leader of the
Fascist movement.

Dislodged from Fiume when his headquarters was shelled by an
Italian gunboat and almost brought down about his ears, D'Annunzio
then retired to the quieter shores of Lake Garda in the north of Italy.
Here he purchased the Villa Cargnacco that later became the Vittoriale
degli Italiani and is now a national museum and repository of the
writer's library, archives, and personal and literary mementoes. In the
years between Mussolini's coming to power in 1922 and D'Annunzio's
death in 1938, the head of the Fascist state was careful to keep a
wary but sympathetic eye on the Comandante in his golden cage at

Garda. Although he once declared D'Annunzio the sort of "genius suitable for exceptional moments rather than for everyday politics,"[3] Mussolini also took pains to keep the aging writer and hero under respectful surveillance at Il Vittoriale while at the same time playing to his vanity by such gestures of official esteem as naming him Prince of Montenevoso, assuming the considerable expenses for the modernization and (sometimes grotesque) renovation of his villa, and underwriting the publication of the "National Edition" of his writings.

D'Annunzio the Memorialist

The mostly autobiographical prose D'Annunzio wrote in France and Italy before and after Fiume has a more subdued tone, employs a less complex syntax, and tends to place less emphasis on the exceptional man than did his earlier work in whatever genre. The fictionalized diaries, reminiscences, and other writings that make up this group of compositions thus represent a new direction for his writing. Imbued with a greater sense of the fragility of existence and an increased awareness of the limitations of even the most dramatic human life, D'Annunzio's last works were conceived by their author not as tools for domination but as subtle and sometimes ambiguous instruments for the probing of otherwise inaccessible levels of his own mind and memories. "Life," D'Annunzio wrote in 1916, "is not an abstraction . . . but a kind of diffused sensuality, a knowledge available to all of the senses, a substance good to smell, to feel, and to eat" (*Prose*, 1.307). The goal of the late writings is to establish contact with this mysterious, sensual substance and in so doing to determine the limits of writing as a way of knowing rather than a mode of doing.

Solus ad solam

Solus ad solam is one of the most unusual of all of D'Annunzio's books. Its title means "from one (masculine) to one (feminine)"—a phrase that emphasizes the gender and singularity of both the writer and the supposed recipient of his message. Neither a novel nor, as recent research has revealed, an exact transcription of lived experience,[4] the book is made up of journal entries dated over a period of twenty-eight days from 8 September to 4 October 1908. The entries, which are mostly in the present tense and vary in length from a few phrases to several paragraphs, present an account of the dramatic events that marked the end of D'Annunzio's love affair with the Countess Giuseppina Mancini. This affair, which ranks as one of the more important in the long list of such adventures in the life of this notorious rake, lasted for about twenty months, from February 1907 until the autumn of 1908. Several years later, by which time he was living in France and embroiled with Mancini's successor, D'Annunzio sent the manuscript back to his ex-lover in Florence, presumably for her to do as she chose with it. For nearly twenty-five years the countess did nothing. Then, in 1939, just one year after the poet's death, *Solus ad solam* appeared in the bookstores, edited and with an introduction by Jolanda de Blasi. At some later date before her death in 1961—or at least so say her heirs, who have further specified that she was acting at the express order of Pope Pius XII—D'Annunzio's "Giusini" burned the original manuscript that describes her love affair with him, apparently as an act of repentance. Although D'Annunzio never authorized publication of *Solus ad solam,* he did utilize material in it for his account of the madness and ruin of Isabella Inghirami in the final chapters of *Forse che sì forse che no.*

Solus ad solam is described by its narrator as a "book of pain and madness, of desperation and of love" (*Prose,* 3.717). The story it tells actually happened and all of the characters in it appear with their own names. During the summer of 1908, after she had decided to separate from her husband, Count Lorenzo Mancini, in order to be with her lover permanently, Giusini began to be increasingly distressed by feelings of guilt about her behavior. In early September while D'Annunzio was attending an automobile race in Bologna, she left her house in Florence and wandered in a state of extreme agitation through the streets of the city. During this time she fell into the clutches of two obscure individuals who seem to have profited from the distraught woman's confusion to take some sort of advantage of her. By the time she was released, the countess's agitation had become a full-fledged nervous breakdown, and she now refused to leave her house and accused D'Annunzio of being her enemy rather than the concerned lover that he insisted he was. Despite his claims of continued affection for her, the countess's liaison with the famous poet was over.

In *Solus ad solam* D'Annunzio describes his trip from Bologna and arrival back in Florence just minutes too late to rescue Giusini from her abductors, and his subsequent attempts to find out what had happened to her during and after her kidnapping. The book, which is written in the first person and at several points is addressed directly to

Giuseppina, is both a journal addressed to this woman and a kind of detective story in which the narrator makes inquiries at the police station, interviews witnesses, and consults with the victim's doctor. It is also automythography of an especially narcissistic sort. Even though *Solus ad solam* begins with the narrator asserting that "I am writing in order to see clearly within and around me," the text that follows seems more concerned with describing D'Annunzio's own discomfort and bewilderment and providing justifications for his actions than with discovering the real nature and causes of Giuseppina's breakdown. There are even journal entries describing encounters with two other women, one of whom the narrator takes to bed as a surrogate for Giuseppina the way Andrea Sperelli had done in *Il piacere*.

Beyond its significance as an attempt to witness lived experience and thus subordinate and control life through art, *Solus ad solam* is of considerable stylistic importance within D'Annunzio's production. Its diary form, intimate tone, frequently fragmented sentences, un-Supermanlike pessimism, and introspective thrust (though in varying degrees of good faith) make it typical of the late, memorialistic work. In his account of his painful and ultimately destructive love affair with Giuseppina Mancini, the diaphragm separating art and life has become thinner and more penetrable than ever; in his readiness to scrutinize certain unpleasant and shameful aspects of his experience D'Annunzio has moved significantly away from the supremacist poses that characterized his earlier writing.

Contemplazione della morte

Contemplazione della morte (Contemplation of death) of 1912 is also about a mystery: the mystery of death, and attendant enigmas of faith, loneliness, and friendship. Its four chapters—which are again dated in the manner of journal entries, this time over a ten-day period in April 1912—were composed while D'Annunzio was living on the Atlantic coast of France at Arcachon. It was first published in installments in the well-known Milanese newspaper, *Corriere della sera*. While D'Annunzio had begun his career writing for the racy Roman periodicals of the "Byzantine" era, toward the end of his life he turned increasingly to the rather different pages of this socially and politically conservative paper. Many of the autobiographical sketches produced for the *Corriere* were published under the title of *Faville del maglio* or "Sparks from the Blacksmith's Hammer." Although this implies that such work was a kind of by-product thrown off by an artistic forge whose main energies were directed elsewhere, D'Annunzio's *"sfavillare"* ("sparkling"), as he somewhat disparagingly called this writing, was not only a reliable source of income for him while in France, it also constituted some of his most significant literary activity during this period.

Contemplazione della morte is dedicated to two people for whom D'Annunzio had complicated and sometimes ambivalent feelings of affection and respect and whose deaths took place almost simultaneously: the Italian poet Giovanni Pascoli, and D'Annunzio's landlord and friend at Arcachon, Adolphe Bermond. The opening section of the book contains descriptions of two meetings between D'Annunzio and Pascoli. After Carducci's death in 1906 Pascoli was the only living Italian poet whose stature was comparable to that of D'Annunzio. Although D'Annunzio had concluded his *Alcyone* with a dedication to him as a poetic "brother" and "the last offspring of Virgil" ("Il commiato," 115), he was never quite at ease when in the company of his poetic "sibling," as is apparent from this part of the book.

The rest of *Contemplazione della morte* tells the story of D'Annunzio's friendship with the octogenarian and fervent Catholic Adolphe Bermond. In this account the pious and gentle Bermond, who in the period in question was slowly dying of stomach cancer, is determined, though with great tact and delicacy, to bring the Italian writer to the same faith that was sustaining him in his final hours. Although deeply touched by his admirer's concern and moved by the courage with which he faces his illness, D'Annunzio finally rejects the possibility of finding consolation in religion, though he vows to follow his friend's example and confront his own end in such a way that his death too will be a "beautiful victory" (*Prose*, 3.282).

In the course of his eschatological meditations D'Annunzio finds occasion to quote at length from the two plays that he was working on at the time, the *Martyre de Saint Sébastien* and *La Parisina,* and to evoke a number of incidents from his earlier life and travels. But it is the theme of death that dominates this journal just as it was madness that dominated *Solus ad solam.* Toward the end of the *Contemplazione della morte* the narrator comes upon the corpse of a drowned man that has been washed up on the beach near his quarters. In passages that stress the carnal and consequently fragile nature of the human envelope, the image of this drowning victim assumes an iconic value for the narrator who finds he is unable to dismiss it from his mind. The book closes, however, with a figure of animal vitality much favored in D'Annunzio's personal symbolism, that of the greyhounds that he was breeding and racing in France at this time. In this episode newborn puppies from D'Annunzio's kennel are given for nursing to a nonpedigreed bitch whose recently whelped offspring have been drowned so that she can provide more milk for her new charges. Although the poet deplores the pointless slaughter of the mongrel puppies, the point seems to be that art and the artist must be served, even at such a cost. Pascoli's and Bermond's deaths, like those of the puppies and the drowned man, have at least given life to the book that D'Annunzio has written.

Proem to the *Vita di Cola di Rienzo*

In 1913 D'Annunzio reprinted a biography of the fourteenth-century political agitator and one-time Tribune of Rome, Cola di Rienzo, that he had published earlier in the magazine *Rinascimento*. In his new proem to this *Vita di Cola di Rienzo* D'Annunzio explains some of his views on biography, especially the importance of peripheral details for the understanding of a man's life, and discourses at length on his love for the archaic Tuscan lexicon as codified in the famous *Vocabolario* or dictionary of the Accademia della Crusca (begun 1612). Throughout this introduction the language employed has been made to conform to that approved by the Crusca Academy, so much so that the language itself of D'Annunzio's discourse becomes the real subject of the work, signified and signifier merge, and the text's meaning is its own textuality.

La Leda senza cigno

La Leda senza cigno (Leda without the swan) was also written at Arcachon and first appeared in installments in the *Corriere della sera,* in this case during the summer of 1913. Like *Solus ad solam* and *Contemplazione della morte,* it too is written in the first person, though not in the form of a journal. *La Leda senza cigno* is a short story of the "frame" variety in that its principal, first-person discourse is set off or framed by an introduction and conclusion written by a second narrator. Although there seems to have been a precedent in D'Annunzio's experience for the events of this story, the characters who appear in it all have fictitious names and its episodes do not have the same immediate relationship to their author's life that they did in other work of this period.

La Leda senza cigno is the story of a beautiful but vampirelike woman whose exterior attractiveness conceals an inner reality that fascinates and terrifies the narrator, Desiderio Moriar. Moriar sees this woman for the first time at a concert in an episode that serves as pretext for a virtuoso prose performance by D'Annunzio. As Moriar listens, the Scarlatti sonata being performed is given a number of visual equivalents including pearls bouncing down marble staircases, preening peacocks that rush to gobble up the pearls as if they were grain, and a clutter of Angora cats that are "white as cream and gray as smoke, with red or light blue eyes," that vie with the peacocks and a troop of black monkeys for the cascading jewels (*Romanzi,* 2.1198). At the end of his story Desiderio Moriar manages to escape destruction by the mystery woman. However, since he has not succeeded in breaching her inner reality, the "Sconosciuta" or "Unknown," as he calls her, remains as elusive for him as the mythological character who inspired a statue of Leda and the swan that he was reminded of when he saw her embracing one of his greyhounds. This statue, he goes on, was once on display in the Florence Bargello but has since been broken and was only a copy of a lost Leonardo drawing in the first place. Just as Desiderio has been unable to comprehend the true nature of the beautiful women he meets in this story, so art, the tale would seem to indicate, is itself nothing more than a palimpsest of an infinitely receding and finally ungraspable reality that disappears into erasure the more it is contemplated. D'Annunzio's visual equivalents are not the Scarlatti sonata; there is no swan in the story.

Notturno

The problem of the ineffable is important too in *Notturno* (Nocturne) of 1921, the most celebrated of all the compositions in this group of autobiographical writings. This text owes its existence to an accident that occurred during the war when an airplane carrying D'Annunzio made a forced landing and the poet hit his forehead against a machine-gun mount. As a result of this injury, D'Annunzio lost his right eye and was compelled to spend two months confined to his bed. Flat on his back and with both eyes bandaged in a darkened room on Venice's Grand Canal, the recuperating poet wrote the *Notturno* between February and April of 1916, inscribing its individual sentences on "more than ten thousand" narrow strips of paper that were then deciphered and transcribed by his daughter Renata. After some additional editing by its author—one authority speaks of a "vast reelaboration" of the material[5]—the *Notturno* was published by Treves in 1921. The book sold extremely well, in part because of its author's considerable post-Fiume celebrity.

By the time of his accident the springs of the poetry that had gushed so fruitfully for D'Annunzio just a few years earlier had begun to run dry. His project for an Italian national theater was at an end too, as were his experiments with the novel. With the disappearance from his life of Natalia de Goloubeff, the last of his great love affairs was also over, and the Comandante, particularly when compared to the brash and gregarious young aviators he had come to know during the war, was an old and increasingly solitary man. Although D'Annunzio's so-called "nocturnal" phase—the distinction is between the autobiographical work of this period and such "solar" earlier writing as *Canto novo* and *Alcyone*—really began while he was living in France before the war, it was at least partly in response to the personal, artistic, and political disappointments of the postwar years that D'Annunzio threw himself into this final period of literary experimentation.

The *Notturno* is divided into three "Offerte" or "Offerings," plus a concluding note on the circumstances of its composition. The first "Offerta" is set in a lugubrious Venice swaddled in fog and with the echoes of an unhappy war in the distance. Much of this part of the book is given over to a description of the death and funeral of one of the writer's most cherished companions, the aviator Giuseppe Miraglia. The vigil over this man's corpse, a duty D'Annunzio discharged with heroic constancy, is described in considerable detail—right on down to the smell of the putrefying body and the welding of the seams of the lead casket in which Miraglia was placed for burial in a Venetian cemetery. The section concludes with this paragraph:

As I write in the darkness my chain of thought is broken and my hand comes to a stop. The strip of paper I had folded over earlier rises up and falls back on my fingers without making a sound. A shudder of fear runs over me. And I keep completely still, my whole body rigid, not daring to trace a single sign in the shadows. (*Prose,* 1.226)

Signs traced in darkness; death, writing, silence, and fear; the body and imagination besieged by memory and struggling with "the shadows"—these are the kinds of topics that now engage D'Annunzio's imagination.

In *Notturno*'s second "Offerta" the interlacing of the layers of discourse becomes denser as narrative strata from the recent and distant past are joined with present experience. As the writer lies convalescent on his bed, the acoustic and olfactory sensations that strike his heightened sensibilities mix with memories of flights over enemy territory and torpedo-boat trips in dangerous waters, of vacations with Duse to the Tuscan shore, and a trip to Pescara and his mother before the war began. In the "Third Offering" there are additional memories of life in France, horseback rides across the Egyptian desert, and childhood days in the Abruzzi—all of these mixed together with reports from the war zone and the sounds and smells of life outside the window. In this part of the book D'Annunzio's suffering body has become "diaphanous," a kind of projection screen for sensations that are at once corporeal and spiritual, present and remembered, real and hallucinatory (357).

What in a preceding work had been only its contemplation, in the *Notturno* becomes the visceral realization of the reality of bodily dis-solution both before and after death. D'Annunzio's response to the existential horror he feels at the thought of life's termination is twofold in this book. On the one hand, he has become attached to life's quiddity as never before. The book is full of such descriptions of the tiny details of everyday existence as the sounds of the water slapping against the banks of the canal or the fragrances of flowers brought into the sickroom or recalled from the hothouse of the invalid's memory.

In addition, D'Annunzio is now acutely aware that the words he is writing can serve as a hedge against the darkness that he feels increasingly closing in upon him and that even the frenetic political activism of his preceding years has been unable to keep at bay. In this book the distinctions between life and art, the real and the fictive, testimony and fantasy, fact and hallucination have been abolished as never before. The confessional discourse presented by this text, which is again in the first person and mostly in the present tense, purports to derive straight from the writer's unconscious. "I am writing," the narrator says, "like a man casting anchor, with the anchor chain running ceaselessly into a bottomless sea, the flukes finding nothing to grasp, and the chain never coming taut" (181). While the fathomless ocean D'Annunzio claims to be plumbing here is surely the sea of his unconscious, it should not be supposed that this canniest of autobiographers, in a book that was heavily edited five years after its composition, is presenting an unmediated, artless representation of his inner life. The *Notturno* should be understood as a nonmimetic and self-justifying representation that is its own psychological referent, a set, as a recent critic has put it, of "fantastic icons, relics of an epiphany aimed at showing the inaccessibility of things," whose prime function is that of "sacred utterances . . . parts of a magic spell to strengthen the individual's connection to the clan and to protect him from the devastating force of historical becoming."[6] What makes the *Notturno* different from many of D'Annunzio's previous works, especially when considered from a political point of view, is that in it the dreams of domination that have always been essential to his political and sexual ideology have been temporarily set aside. In the *Notturno* the narrator has himself become an object—forced, as Anco Marzio Mutterle says, "to be the register of visions and images whether he wants to or not," and so compelled to realize that "the miracle of creating metamorphoses is not specific to art alone but intrinsic to matter and to life itself."[7] Nature, that obverse side of Alcyone's "two-faced god," clearly shares in the demiurgic powers that this author had previously thought were reserved for art alone.

The *Licenza* to *La Leda senza cigno*

The *Licenza* which accompanied *La Leda senza cigno* when it was published in a volume was written shortly after the first draft of the *Notturno*. Although parts of it had appeared in 1914 as "Faville" for the *Corriere della sera,* and others are from notebook entries made in France, the work as a whole was composed in the spring and summer of 1916 in the same house on the Grand Canal where D'Annunzio had just completed the "more than ten thousand strips" of the *Notturno*.

Though it too is written in the first person, the *Licenza* or "Envoy" to *La Leda senza cigno* has little apparent relation to the story that precedes it in the Treves volume. Its first section contains descriptions of D'Annunzio's life in France during the German invasion in 1914. The mood is one of desperation and shame at such acts of military vandalism as the burning of the cathedral at Reims—an event that D'Annunzio did not actually see, as he pretends here, but cobbled together from the eyewitness accounts of others. Most of the French episodes in this section are juxtaposed with analogous fragments set in Italy—all as part of D'Annunzio's hortatory strategy for a common, "Latin" front against the barbarian menace.

All of the second part of the book takes place in Italy, for the most part in Venice where "Chiaroviso"—that is, Suzanne Boulenger, the wife of the French dandy and man of letters Marcel Boulenger and the woman to whom the text is dedicated—had come with a friend to visit the recuperating poet. Included in this section is some authorial commentary on the *Notturno* and *La Leda senza cigno,* several descriptions of Venetian scenes, and a number of lyrical accounts of the writer's wartime flying experiences. In the military reminiscences the tone is mostly subdued and elegiac though not without occasional bursts of the old patriotic fervor. What D'Annunzio hopes to achieve in this work, however, is "a certain inner nudity . . . an absence of images and of melody, so that the soul can imitate that dawn transparency where 'night and day run together' " (*Romanzi,* 2.1306–7). Unlike the short story with which it is paired in the Treves volume, the *Licenza* to *La Leda senza cigno* has no easily discernible plot or rhetorical form beyond that of its author's remembering imagination. But it is this structure of the imagination that from now on is increasingly the shaping force of D'Annunzio's memorialistic and mythographic prose.

The *Faville del maglio*

Mention has already been made of the sketches that D'Annunzio produced in France for the *Corriere della sera* and titled *Faville del maglio* or "Sparks from the Blacksmith's Hammer." During the first decade of his residence at Il Vittoriale, D'Annunzio collected and published two volumes of these essays. The first, dated 1924, was subtitled *Il venturiero senza ventura e altri studii del vivere inimitabile* (The luckless adventurer and other studies in inimitable living); the second, which saw the light in 1928, *Il compagno degli occhi senza cigli* (The buddy whose eyes had no eyelashes). In the collections the original *Corriere* articles have been retouched, in some cases expanded, and are accompanied by additional work produced for the occasion.[8]

The individual essays that make up the *Faville del maglio* come from several different phases of D'Annunzio's writing career, in some cases deriving from notebook entries made before the turn of the century while others were written from scratch at Il Vittoriale. In an introductory note to the first volume D'Annunzio makes it clear that all of the work he is presenting has been "daringly extracted from the book of my memory," and goes on to explain that, unlike such other memory writers as Petrarch in the *Secretum,* he does not suffer from false modesty. If an earlier poetry collection was a *Laus vitae* or "Praise of Life," these essays constitute a "Laus mei" or "Praise of me" and were written "a chiarezza di me"—that is, for the clarification (though another possible translation is "glorification") of their author.

The *Faville del maglio,* then, constitute an important response by D'Annunzio to the autobiographical imperative that he felt with increasing insistence toward the end of his life and are a repository for what he felt would be his enduring myths as qualified by the events of his last years. In "Il venturiero senza ventura," for example, a composition dated 29 August 1898, D'Annunzio contrasts a present with little scope or appreciation for personal heroism with the glorious Italian Renaissance when an "adventurer" could respond to his "besieging lust" by conquering a city. When this essay appeared among the collected essays of 1924, it could hardly be lost on the readers of that volume that what in 1898 had been only a dream of conquest and glory, by 1919 and the Comandante's occupation of Fiume had become a reality.

Several essays in these volumes use the far limits of old age as a reference point from which to scrutinize the writer's infancy and youth. These essays, however, are not so much case studies of what actually happened to their author as a boy as they are mountings for the carefully furnished signs of D'Annunzio's predestination as a literary and political genius. This strategy is evident, for example, in the episode in *Il secondo amante di Lucrezia Buti* (Lucrezia Buti's second lover) describing how D'Annunzio cut his hand on a jackknife when still a small boy in Pescara. In this account the accident takes on heroic overtones as the wounded lad first devours the mollusk that he was trying to open with the knife, then stifles his tears and impulse to faint, braves the darkness of an abandoned warehouse where he finds spiderwebs to staunch the wound, and finally wobbles home to his mother, bloody but awed by this "first sign of destiny impressed on my mind, the first secret mark of my predestination" (*Prose,* 2.185). In this episode the writer's body has become the medium for the inscriptions of destiny as the sign left by the past persists as a scar on the hand of the mature man tracing his origins in writing.

The most celebrated episodes from D'Annunzio's youth and childhood are contained in the two long essays, *Il secondo amante di Lucrezia Buti* and *Il compagno degli occhi senza cigli,* found in the first and second volumes respectively. In the descriptions they contain of his student days at the Cicognini, D'Annunzio reveals how he kept at the top of his class through his "nocturnal strategy for winning"—that is, his habit of studying through the night while his companions slept.

His disdain for the school's disciplinary code and his genius for cir-cumventing or shattering its rules are presented as foreshadowings of the writer's more methodically transgressive tactics later. In the same way, his success as a leader of schoolboy uprisings seems a premonition of Fiume just as his theft of a pelican wingbone from the school museum and his rooftop escapades after being confined to an upstairs detention room prefigure his wartime aviation adventures.

A number of these essays also treat the theme of sexual awakening—an issue of no small importance for this future master of seduction. In "Il grappolo del pudore" (Grapes of shame) the adolescent D'Annunzio pursues the peasant girl "Sblendore" or "Splendor" who smears her face with grape-squeezings in order to evade his grasp but in doing so only renders herself more maenadic and thus desirable to the vacationing classics scholar. "La chimera e l'altra bocca" (The chimera and the other mouth) takes place in the Etruscan museum in Florence where the young schoolboy twice dares fate: once by placing his hand in the forbidden mouth-hole of an Etruscan mask and then by kissing and fondling his female companion. A similar contamination of ancient myth and modern lust is described in "La spelonca di Dido" (Dido's cave) where a passage in Virgil goads the inflamed adolescent to accelerate his plans to lose his virginity. When the young D'Annunzio goes for this purpose to a Florentine brothel, he cannot resist imagining himself as a Napoleonic hero and mentally transforms the kindly but ordinary prostitute he finds there into the Quattrocento beauty Lucrezia Buti as painted by the artist, Fra Filippo Lippi.

In all these episodes the remembering D'Annunzio stresses the analogies he sees between incidents of sexual and literary initiation. Although many of these episodes are included here as portents of D'Annunzio's destiny as the lover of Europe's most desirable women, the most authentic and enduring love affair of these pages is that between the ambitious provincial schoolboy and the Tuscany to which he emigrated and where he first came into contact with the linguistic tools he needed to become the person he really was. The essays that describe his student days at the Cicognini are filled with his admiration for the Tuscan landscape, Tuscan art, and Tuscan history, and especially with tales of D'Annunzio's conquests of the Tuscan language and the tutors who had at first intimidated him with it. For it was always language and writing that satisfied the deepest—and the most corporeal—of this writer's needs. In the aptly titled "Vivo, scrivo" (I live, I write) from *Il secondo amante di Lucrezia Buti* D'Annunzio describes the relationship that has always applied between his body and his writing:

How long have I been writing? I should say, how long have I been living. . . . I live, I write. My veins throb, my lungs breathe, my pen moves, in the same continuous mystery, the same measured miracle, the same inimitable game. For me writing is a need to reveal myself, a need for renown not unlike the need to breathe, the need for my heart to beat, to march down the roads of the earth toward the unknown. For me writing is obedience to a profound law of my being. Writing is discerning a glimmer of my secret truth underneath my fleeting and changeable character. The least of my cadences can help me understand the nature of my strength—more than the motions of my pulse or the rhythms of my breathing. This power of expression and representation is so assiduous, potent, and impatient within me that it is sometimes enough to hear a distant cry in the field, a flutter of wings in the sky, a splashing of water in a ditch for my whole life suddenly to rise up and marvelously and irresistibly strive to take on artistic form. (*Prose,* 2.390–91)

Libro segreto

A preoccupation with writing, the body, and the slippery entity of the self also runs through much of the *Libro segreto* (Secret book) or—to give it its full title—*Cento e cento e cento e cento pagine del libro segreto di Gabriele D'Annunzio tentato di morire* (A hundred and a hundred and a hundred and a hundred pages of the secret book of Gabriele D'Annunzio tempted to die). Published under the transparent pseudonym of Angelo Cocles just three years before D'Annunzio's death, the *Libro segreto* of 1935 is his last composition of consequence to be published during his lifetime.[9]

By the time he brought out this work, D'Annunzio was living in seclusion at Il Vittoriale, in ill health and with his spirits alternatingly sagging at the thought of his physical deterioration and soaring in conviction of his own greatness. Although parts of the book seem to have been composed in the years just preceding its publication, the *Libro segreto* was more assembled from already existing material than composed afresh at this time; most of it is made up of fragments and notations on a variety of subjects that D'Annunzio had taken down at intervals over the years and then gathered together for the occasion. The book is organized into two sections: a linearly organized autobiographical first part called *Via crucis Via necis Via nubis* (Way of the cross, way of death, way of mist), and a second, more chaotic, and topically inconsistent section titled *Regimen hinc animae* (This is the realm of the soul).

In the *Libro segreto* D'Annunzio again meditates on the meaning of his life, particularly in the light of an old age that has increasingly reduced him to little more than a "pale sack of salty water." Peeping out from behind the mask that he realizes is concealing both his own face and that of others, he finds he can sum up the experiences of his life in the following set of phrases:

The boarding school of the Cicogna—the conquest of Rome—the need for a heroic example—Tuscan days, Roman days, exile days—the sense of a wasted life—inescapable old age—the empty grave—the glory that survives, the multitude's vile fickleness and the empty, filthy chatter of public opinion— *me luridus occupat horror* (the ghastly horror overwhelms me). (*Prose*, 2.742–43)

But instead of buckling under to this horror, D'Annunzio is determined to obey the injunction of "Carpe diem" or "Seize the day." Is "ascetic discipline" the answer? His response is to persevere in the demiurgic effort that has always been part of his artistic credo—"to draw every thing, every event, every appearance into my art, into my arts." "This," he concludes, "is my law" (743).

Although the frequent Greek and Latin phrases in this book indicate that D'Annunzio is convinced that he is carrying forward an illustrious literary tradition that stretches back for more than a millenium, the author of the *Libro segreto* is aware as never before of the inadequacy of even the greatest literary art to represent the "black abyss of the heart" or render through written signs the nature of the interaction between human interiority and the outside world:

The great art of antiquity, like the modern, flees the black abyss of the heart and reduces itself to the representation through material signs of attitudes and gestures. How miserable are the signs of even the greatest poet when compared to his sensibility, his intuition, and the mystery he is constantly breathing! . . . To represent the inner man and invisible forces, an art of the word must be created that is based on the total abolition of literary habits. . . . The soul's most secret communication with things cannot be captured, at least not yet, except in pauses, for these are the words of silence. . . . There is absolutely no congruence between our real, hidden life and the words used to elaborate it. (777–78)

At the very end of his life D'Annunzio has become excruciatingly aware of the inadequacy of his art to express the things that really matter. Now that death was upon him, the Medusa face of the ineffable and its challenge to representation seemed more cruel and more mocking than ever. Madness, suicide, artistic and sexual impotence, above all an unhappy sense that there was no time left for him: these are the great themes of this last book. "Now that I finally know what the essence of art is," he says with melancholy arrogance in another place, "now that I have attained mastery, now that after fifty books I have learned how a book should be made, now I have only the evening of tomorrow to express myself completely, the evening of tomorrow to sing my new *Canto novo* and delude myself that I am happy" (896).

In his secret book of dreams, insomniac musings, memories of happier times, and fears of the future D'Annunzio has become aware as never before of the weight as well as the pleasure of being a public personality, the "ferocious *taedium vitae* . . . the irritation—that today is almost the horror—of having been and of being Gabriele D'Annunzio, bound to the existence of the man, the artist, the hero Gabriele D'Annunzio, constrained to a past and bound to a future of this existence: of certain words said, certain pages written, certain acts declared and accomplished: *erotica heroica*" (922). One way to slip the constraints of his public identity as "man, artist, and hero" is for D'Annunzio to conceal himself behind a mask. As he says in another place: "the darkness grows thicker, the anguish tighter. Do I perhaps want to deceive them both by forcing my writer's mask upon my distorted face?" (777). If his identity as a writer is no more than a mask of an inner, inaccessible reality, then writing can never reveal the truth of the human condition. "A poet's soul can possess things the same way that it possesses love, hate, or hope. But in the act of expressing these things it ceases to possess them. It is language that makes external what had been an intimate part of the poet's soul" (780). Not only is language doomed to failure in its attempt to express the most "intimate part of the poet's soul," D'Annunzio's own essence can never be captured in words, either his or those of others. As he remarks in a passage that occurs with variants in two different places in this book:

Who, today and in the centuries to come, will ever be able to guess that part of me that I have wanted to conceal? There is an inhuman pleasure [in the variant, a "bitter pleasure"] in being unknown and in behaving in such a way as to remain unknown. Inhuman? Perhaps divine. Perhaps I am

the only one who knows this. I alone truly know how to savor and renew
this pleasure. (727, 918)

Locked within his private self and compelled to rely only on the
untrustworthy medium of language to express what he finds there, at
the end of this book D'Annunzio falls back on the bitter sneer already
quoted here in regard to *Giovanni Episcopo:*

> Tutta la vita è senza mutamento
> Ha un solo volto la malinconia.
> Il pensiere ha per cima la follia.
> E l'amore è legato a tradimento.
>
> (926)

> [All of life is monotony.
> Melancholy has just one face.
> Madness is thought's highest place.
> And love is bound to treachery.]

Chapter Seven

The Inimitable

In addition to the poetry collections, novels, plays, memoirs, and autobiographical writings discussed in the preceding chapters, D'Annunzio left a large number of speeches and political correspondence, some important notebooks (the *Taccuini* and *Altri taccuini* [Notebooks and More notebooks]) published by Bianchetti and Forcella in 1965 and 1976, and a vast number of letters of all sorts which even today remain mostly unpublished. One way to conceptualize this writer's work is as a series of consecutive and interlinked parabolas or rising and falling arcs moving across time. The first such arc is made up of two superimposed curves, one configuring the derivative but increasingly autonomous poetry of the 1880s and 1890s, the other the naturalistic stories and journalistic prose and fables of the same period. A second, intersecting parabola represents the decade of the novels from *Il piacere* of 1889 to *Il fuoco* of 1900, with *Forse che sì forse che no* of 1910 a later bulge in the arc. This parabola is intersected by the curve of the plays, a literary activity that began just as the prose fiction was beginning to come to an end and continued on up to the war with its irresistible call to another kind of action and the testing of the exceptionality that D'Annunzio had always insisted lay at his personal core.

Inside the parabola formed by the plays is the brief, soaring arc of the *Laudi* and *Alcyone,* poetry that D'Annunzio had been moving toward from the beginning of his career and that continued to loom in his past long after the incandescently fertile period of those volumes. Finally, encompassing all of these minor curves is the parabola of the memorialistic writing. The arc representing this activity begins to rise with D'Annunzio's first printed utterances and reaches its zenith during the final years of reflection and intensified automythography at Garda as the aged writer struggled to adjust his nearly completed personal fable to fit the outlines of the heroic and exemplary story whose definitive shape he was finally able to perceive.

What is unusual about D'Annunzio's activity as a writer—and it is what has always been remarked about him and his work—is the restless experimentalism that the arching of these consecutive parabolas represents.

Despite his repeated assertions and hyperbolic exaltation of the quality of his written work, especially in such books as the *Libro segreto,* D'Annunzio's sharp sense throughout his career of the imperative to renew oneself or perish—"o rinnovarsi o morire"—suggests a perpetual dissatisfaction with all of his writing and an uncertainty about the relationship between that writing and his most private identity. Throughout his life D'Annunzio was deeply concerned with adjusting his past work, both published and unpublished, to make it fit into a pattern of human and literary significance that became evident to him only in retrospect.

This self-revision of the content, significance, and sometimes the style of his literary production, and thus of his public and private identity, gets under way as early as *Primo vere.* It will be recalled that this volume was corrected "with pen and fire" just one year after its first appearance—and at the cost, in effect, of killing off the volume's original creator since the second edition was marketed simultaneously with the announcement of its adolescent author's untimely demise. The middle books of poetry underwent similar revisions. The naughty *Intermezzo di rime* of 1884 was reissued in 1894 with new instructions for use as a book of repentance and literary initiation; the lavishly produced *Isaotta Gottadàura ed altre poesie* of 1886 was redone in 1890 with additional poems and no illustrations; above all there is the *Canto novo* of 1882 reproposed in 1896 as a still newer "new song" and anticipation of *Alcyone.* All of these rereadings and revisions reveal an author who has become aware only afterward of the significance and intentions of his earlier work and character, and is willing to change that record of who he was to meet the claims of his evolving sense of his own identity.

D'Annunzio's invariably autobiographical novels too, even though for the most part they were not issued in revised editions, can be considered revisions or corrections: in their case, of lived experience bereft of meaning until realized as fiction. This is true even for such a book as *Solus ad solam* which, anything but a faithful mirror of the Mancini/ D'Annunzio affair in the first place, was further corrected and transformed in the closing episode of *Forse che sì, forse che no* into something quite different from what it had been in the earlier work. Such more explicit memory books as the *Faville del maglio, Notturno,* and *Libro segreto,* with their automythographic approach to their author's infancy, childhood, and war experiences, are further examples of D'Annunzio's inability to resist the temptation to transform history into legend and life into literature. So too his tinkering with the "national edition" of his complete works—his assigning new titles to the sections in which the earlier writings are grouped, his projecting additional, as yet unwritten further works, and his renaming already-written compositions for their inclusion in this new context—is a result of D'Annunzio's continued rage to assign shape and significance to his existence as writer, man, and finally legend by constantly reviewing and editing his own record of his life and career.

D'Annunzio's untiring assemblage, disassemblage, and re-creation of these representations of himself suggest that the significance he wishes to give his work is located somewhere beyond the boundaries of the individual texts themselves. Since, for D'Annunzio, the writer is compelled to stave off his death as an artist by perpetually "renewing himself" in an incessant erasure of past styles and identities, so too his writing calls out to be revised and rewritten almost as soon as it has achieved tentative closure. In his own view D'Annunzio is not an author of discrete texts tied to precise moments in the historical continuum, but a demiurgic creator of a single metatext disassociated from historical time whose individual passages and episodes flow into one another through quotations, duplications, corrections, and cross-references. In this sense D'Annunzio is not a writer of individual books at all but a disseminator of a vast, interlaced life text fabricated not only in the writing studio where he often wore out sheaves of goose quill pens in a compositional frenzy, but in such other private and public contexts as the Roman and Parisian boudoirs he so spectacularly favored, and the trenches and skies of World War I where he embraced a different kind of reality.

A central topic of the life text that D'Annunzio spent his career composing is that of energy, the "tenth muse" not only of *Laus vitae* but of all of his writing. For D'Annunzio, the energy that drives artistic, political, or sexual activity is always the same and cannot be differentiated into separate impulses. Though formulated without reference to Freud's research and writing during these same years (Gibellini muses that D'Annunzio's lack of knowledge of Freud's work constitutes one of the "great missed appointments" of this poet's career),[1] D'Annunzio's ideas about the workings of psychic energy are remarkably similar to his Viennese contemporary's notions of the libido and of artistic activity as sexual sublimation. In some jottings from 1929 that Anna Maria Andreoli discovered among the poet's papers at Il Vittoriale and used as epigraph to her monograph on him, D'Annunzio describes the equivalence of artistic and sexual desire in terms that recall those of Freudian theory,

though transformed by his own tastes for the shocking and transgressive
and his own notions of the connections between writing and the body.
Writing of the creative impulses driving his own artistic activity, D'Annunzio insists that "the sexual instinct, inebriation, and cruelty lie at
the roots of my expressive potency and of my most lofty art." Using
even more explicit terminology, he goes on to say that "the spurt of
my art, the spurt of my poetry, is like the spurt of my semen." For
D'Annunzio, the exercise of power, however mediated by more immediate
considerations, has a single goal. "In sexual desire, heroism, and art,"
he declares, "I wield the same victorious energy that made and makes
Life and Death into a single ideal space."[2] This ideal space—"un solo
spazio ideale della Vita e della Morte" located beyond life and death
in a realm of freedom not subject to temporally defined constrictions—
would seem to be the goal of all of his creative activity.

Unlike many other novelists, D'Annunzio never created truly autonomous characters in his longer fiction. As his earliest readers were quick
to realize and has been universally acknowledged since, the heroes of
D'Annunzio's novels are all autobiographical projections of his own
character and preoccupations. Similarly, his female characters are always
incarnations of their author's desire, the products of his sexual fantasies
rather than depictions of autonomous feminine personalities. Such "Superfemmine" as Ippolita Sanzio or Isabella Inghirami, Basiliola, or Fedra,
are so lacking in verisimilitude as to appear almost ridiculous, protagonists
of the sexual parodies of "high camp" rather than serious literary
personages. This is because such women in D'Annunzio's fiction have
no psychological substance except as representations of their author's
fantasies. And if these strong-minded and passionate but ultimately
lifeless female antagonists frequently threaten D'Annunzio's male protagonists with circumscription or destruction, this is because their real
function in the life text D'Annunzio is creating is to embody authorial
anxieties that center on a female Other indifferent or recalcitrant to the
demands of male desire and solipsistically satisfied instead with her own
impenetrable alterity. It is because his characters are drawn in this way,
from out of the depths of his psyche rather than from observed history
or social practice, that D'Annunzio's novels are often narratively inert
and his plays lack dramatic energy. On the other hand, his poems,
which do not require the same interaction among distinct personalities
for their success, have remained the more readable among his imaginative
works.

For D'Annunzio, the purpose of writing is not to understand or clarify the nature of the world, either to himself or to others. This is why matters of truth or sincerity, falseness or authenticity are not important for him. In "L'otre" (The skin) from the final section of *Alcyone* D'Annunzio spoke through the receptacle of the poem's title to announce:

> Molto contenni, puro o adulterato.
> Il falso e il vero sono le foglie alterne
> d'un ramoscello: il savio non discerne
> l'una dall'altra, l'un dall'altro lato.
> (273–76)

[I contained much, both pure and contaminated. / The true and the false are alternating leaves / on a branch: a wise man does not distinguish / one leaf or one side from the other.]

In the rest of this poem D'Annunzio insists that for a real writer, content is not important. Writing has nothing to do with making sense of the world, but is an activity that one does for oneself. In D'Annunzio's case he wrote to become famous and to make the money that seemed to flow through his hands like the water of the Arno estuary he described in his poetry. In addition, writing, like sex, could also be a way of dominating: first of women, then of audiences in a theater, then of audiences beneath a balcony that soon grew into entire nations. A way of asserting himself in a hostile and unforgiving world, writing was the best way—though finally a tragically ineffective one—D'Annunzio knew of giving a meaning to his life and keeping away the shadows that he sensed on its periphery. It is perhaps this defensive notion of literature as a means to obtain an otherwise impossible though finally illusory mastery that can serve as a point of contact between the determinants of D'Annunzio's artistic activities and the political ideology dominant in his country at the end of his life. In this reading, Fascism not only aped some of the more visible appurtenances of D'Annunzio's style, it recognized and took for its own the motivating emptiness that lay at its core.

Notes and References

Chapter One

1. Henry James, "The Saint's Afternoon and Others," *Italian Hours* (Boston: Houghton Mifflin, 1909), 486.

2. For James's reservations about D'Annunzio, especially his treatment of "the sexual passion" in his novels, see his "Gabriele D'Annunzio," *Notes on Novelists* (New York: Scribner's, 1914), 245–93.

3. For the history and an anthology of D'Annunzio's reception, see Giuseppe Petronio, *D'Annunzio, Storia della critica*, 28 (Palermo: Palumbo, 1977).

4. For Sommaruga, see Richard Drake, *Byzantium for Rome: the Politics of Nostalgia in Umbertian Italy, 1878–1900* (Chapel Hill: University of North Carolina Press, 1980).

5. *Versi d'amore e di gloria*, 2 vols., ed. Annamaria Andreoli and Niva Lorenzini (Milan: Mondadori, 1982–84), 1:189–90. All quotations from D'Annunzio's poetry are from this edition. When the sources of further quotations are not clear from the context, they will be identified in the text by title (book and/or section) and line numbers rather than by page references.

6. All translations of D'Annunzio's writings—whether prose, poetry, or plays—are my own.

7. For the unpublished letter, see Ivanos Ciani, "La nascita dell'idea di *Canto novo*," *Canto novo nel centenario della pubblicazione. Atti del IV Convegno internazionale di studi dannunziani* (Pescara: Centro nazionale di studi dannunziani, 1983), 32.

Chapter Two

1. Edoardo Scarfoglio, *Il libro di Don Chisciotte* (Milan: Mondadori, 1925), 159.

2. Piero Chiara, *Vita di Gabriele D'Annunzio* (Milan: Mondadori, 1978), 51.

3. *Roma senza lupa: cronache mondane, 1884–1888*, ed. A. Baldini and P.P. Trompeo (Milan: Domus, 1948), 196.

4. *Poesie*, ed. Federico Roncoroni (Milan: Garzanti, 1982), 34–35.

5. The phrase is Roncoroni's, ibid., 63.

6. See *Gabriele D'Annunzio, Poesie complete con interpretazione e commento di Enzo Palmieri*, vol. 1, *Primo vere Canto novo Intermezzo* (Bologna: Zanichelli, 1953), 360–71.

7. *Poesia italiana del Novecento,* ed. Edoardo Sanguineti (Turin: Einaudi, 1969), 1:67.

8. Quoted in *Versi d'amore e di gloria,* 1:952.

9. See Emilio Mariano, "Il nuovo di *Canto novo 1896,*" *Canto novo nel centenario,* 182.

Chapter Three

1. At one point D'Annunzio did think about writing a "Homeric-epic" historical novel set in Pescara between 1850 and 1875. See his letter to Nencioni of 6 September 1884 reprinted in *Nuova Antologia* 403 (1 May 1939):19.

2. Anco Marzio Mutterele, *Gabriele D'Annunzio: Introduzione e guida allo studio dell'opera dannunziana* (Florence: Le Monnier, 1982), 53.

3. *Tutte le opere di Gabriele D'Annunzio: Prose di romanzi* (Milan: Mondadori, 1978), 1:17. Unless otherwise specified, all further references to D'Annunzio's prose and plays are to this edition and are cited in the text. They refer to his works as they appear in *Tutte le opere: Tragedie, sogni e misteri,* vols. 1 & 2; *Prose di romanzi* (cited as *Romanzi*), vols. 1 & 2; and *Prose di ricerca, di lotta, ecc.* (cited as *Prose*), vols. 1–3.

4. Luciano Anceschi, "Introduzione," *Versi d'amore e di gloria,* 1:1.

5. D'Annunzio claimed that this was the reaction of the physiologist, Jacob Moleschott (*Prose,* 2.672).

6. Paolo Valesio, "The Lion and the Ass: The Case for D'Annunzio's Novels," *Yale Italian Studies* 1 (1977):75.

7. Quoted in *Prose,* ed. Federico Roncoroni (Milan: Garzanti, 1983), 103.

8. For Hérelle, see Giovanni Gullace, *Gabriele D'Annunzio in France: A Study in Cultural Relations* (Syracuse, N.Y.: Syracuse University Press, 1966).

9. "Atrocious agonies, abject joys, shameful submissions, vile pacts proposed and accepted without a blush, tears more bitter than any poison . . . all the miseries and all the infamies of carnal passion exasperated by jealousy—I knew them all" (*Romanzi,* 405–6).

10. Jacques Goudet, *D'Annunzio romanziere* (Florence: Olschki, 1976), 88–89.

11. See the "Introduzione" by Maria Teresa Giannelli in the "Oscar" edition of Gabriele D'Annunzio, *L'Innocente* (Milan: Mondadori, 1982), 26.

12. Giusi Oddo De Stefanis does not find the novel's story unresolved at all, deeming it a coherent expression of a Nietzschean "death of God," and transcendence of conventional, Christian morality. See her *"L'Innocente: Il mito del superuomo e il mondo della 'trascendenza deviata,'"* *Forum Italicum* 20 (1986):83–99.

13. For this often unfaithful translation, see John Woodhouse, "Il *Trionfo della morte:* traduzioni, reazioni e interpretazioni anglosassoni," *Trionfo della morte. Atti del Terzo Convegno internazionale di studi dannunziani* (Pescara: Centro nazionale di Studi dannunziani, 1983), 239–58.

14. For a brilliant Freudian reading of the novel, see Ubaldo Serbo, "*Il Trionfo della morte:* autobiografia ossessiva di Gabriele D'Annunzio," ibid., 315–24.

15. For a suggestion that D'Annunzio's misogynism here may have been influenced by Otto Weininger's *Sex and Culture,* see the chapter "La volontà d'impotenza" in Arturo Mazzarella, *Il piacere e la morte* (Naples: Liguori, 1983).

16. Mutterle, *Gabriele D'Annunzio,* 66.

17. This is the thesis developed by Roncoroni in the "Introduzione" to his anthologies of D'Annunzio's *Poesie* and *Prose.*

18. For this observation, and much else in regard to this novel, I am indebted to Lucia Re, "D'Annunzio's Novel *Le vergini delle rocce:* 'Una cosa naturale vista in un grande specchio,' " *Stanford Italian Review* 3, no. 7 (Fall, 1983):241–71.

19. For information on both these novel cycles, see Eurialo De Michelis, *Tutto D'Annunzio* (Milan: Feltrinelli, 1960), 168–69.

20. Goudet believes that Cantelmo, and with him D'Annunzio, is employing "the magic of persuasion" to "demystify his fearful adversary, the World," to "convince himself . . . that the seductive and terrible monster that is the Universe is nothing but a shadow, a marvelous production of the creative imagination . . . without external substance. It is in just such a fashion," he continues, "from the primordial fear inherent in any conscious coming to grips with existence, that supermen and gods are born" (*D'Annunzio romanziere,* 193).

21. Guy Tosi, "D'Annunzio découvre Nietzsche (1892–1894)," *Italianistica* 2 (1973):481–513.

22. *Pagine disperse,* ed. Antonio Castelli (Rome: Lux, 1913), 544.

23. Quoted in Paolo Alatri, *D'Annunzio* (Turin: UTET, 1983), 110.

24. William Weaver, *Duse: A Biography* (New York: Harcourt Brace Jovanovich, 1984), 225.

25. Ibid., 241.

26. See De Michelis, *Tutto D'Annunzio,* 204; Alatri, *D'Annunzio,* 208.

27. Roberto Tessari, *Il mito della macchina nella letteratura italiana del primo Novecento* (Milan: Mursia, 1973), 200.

28. Ibid., 201.

Chapter Four

1. In the introduction to his play, *Più che amore* (Milan: Treves, 1906), xlviii.

2. See Guy Tosi, *D'Annunzio en Grèce: Laus vitae et la croisière de 1895* (Paris: Calmann-Lèvy, 1947), and the documentation in *Versi d'amore e di gloria*, 2.875–994.

3. See the article by Lorenzo Braccesi, "Le patrie ideali nel libro di *Maia*: Roma," *Quaderni del Vittoriale* 23 (1980):26–39.

4. The chronology of composition of these poems has been studied by Franco Gavazzeni, *Le sinopie di "Alcione"* (Milan and Naples: Ricciardi, 1980), and by Pietro Gibellini, "La storia di *Alcyone*," now in *Logos e mythos: studi su Gabriele D'Annunzio* (Florence: Olschki, 1985), 31–84. There is a useful tabular summary of the matter in *Alcyone*, ed. Federico Roncoroni (Milan: Mondadori, 1982), 757–65.

5. Two recent studies of *Alcyone*'s lexicon, both with bibliographies, are Pietro Gibellini, "Fiori di carta: la fonte della flora di *Alcyone*," *Logos e mythos*, 133–152, and Paolo Bongrani, "D'Annunzio e i vocabolari: alcuni studi recenti," *Lingua nostra* 44 (1983):57–69.

6. For the relation between the two works see *Versi d'amore e di gloria*, 2.875–912, 1144–1175.

7. Quoted in *Poesie*, ed. Roncoroni, 325–26.

8. For the idea that much modern literature prefers a time other than the workaday for the unfolding of its action, see Frederic Jameson, *Marxism and Form* (Princeton, N.J.: Princeton University Press, 1971), 167.

9. Giorgio Bàrberi Squarotti, *Invito alla lettura di Gabriele D'Annunzio* (Milan: Mursia, 1982), 145.

10. Gibellini, *Logos e mythos*, 128.

Chapter Five

1. D'Annunzio later changed his mind about including the later volume as *Asterope* or *Sterope*, the fifth of the *Laudi* series. For the story of the oscillations of the title given this volume, see *Poesie*, ed. Roncoroni, 563–67.

2. See "Laude dell'illaudato" in *Prose*, 1.468; there is an identical passage in *Il fuoco* (*Romanzi*, 2.660).

3. The first Italian performance, with Duse as Anna, was not until 1901. Both *La città morta* and *La Ville morte* were published in 1898. For first performances and printings of D'Annunzio's plays see, in addition to Alatri and De Michelis, Armand Caraccio, *D'Annunzio dramaturge* (Grenoble: Presses Universitaires de France, 1950), and Renée Lelièvre, *Le Théâtre dramatique italien en France 1855–1940* (Paris: Armand Colin, 1959).

4. See Paolo Scarpi, "L'Edipo negato e la trasformazione del mito," *Quaderni del Vittoriale* 23 (1980):73–99.

5. For a reading of the play as a treatment of the threatened dissolution of the family and the reestablishment of order through death, see Scarpi, ibid.

6. Caraccio, *D'Annunzio dramaturge*, 30.

7. Lelièvre, *Théâtre dramatique*, 188.

8. It seems worth noting in passing that the play is dedicated to "Eleonora Duse of the beautiful hands" and that the motif of mutilated female hands occurs in several places in D'Annunzio's works.

9. Caraccio, for example, while judging *La gloria* "mediocre" as a play, notes that it is also "prophétique" (81); cf. also Alatri, *D'Annunzio*, 204–7.

10. Bàrberi Squarotti, *Invito alla lettura*, 117.

11. Alatri, *D'Annunzio*, 231; *Prose*, ed. Roncoroni, cxxiii.

12. Gibellini, "Introduzione," *Logos e mythos*, 11.

13. Caroccio, *D'Annunzio dramaturge*, 123.

14. See Giovanna Tomasello, "L'eroe dannunziano e l'Africa nella costruzione dell'ideologia coloniale dell'Italia prefascista," *Quaderni del Vittoriale* 36 (1982):111–23.

15. *Prose*, ed. Roncoroni, cxxvii.

16. For these details, see Alatri, *D'Annunzio*, 260.

17. For the Lyons production, see Guy Tosi, "La fortuna del *Martyre de Saint Sébastien* in Francia (1948–1969)," *Quaderni del Vittoriale* 24 (1980):95–99; the playbill and text of the original production were reproduced in *L'Illustration théâtrale* of 27 May 1911.

18. "I write rapidly as if in my native tongue. But I note the distortions of my spirit and sensibility because of this foreign language" (*Prose*, 2.757).

19. Gianfranco Contini, "Vita macaronica del francese dannunziano," *Esercizi di lettura* (Florence: Le Monnier, 1947), 367–84; Guy Tosi, "D'Annunzio écrivain français: Le travail du style dans *Le Martyre de Saint Sébastien*," *Quaderni del Vittoriale* 5–6 (1977):104–39, 139.

Chapter Six

1. Alatri, *D'Annunzio*, 52.

2. See Michael A. Ledeen, *The First Duce: D'Annunzio at Fiume* (Baltimore: Johns Hopkins University Press, 1977), 1.

3. Alatri, *D'Annunzio*, 502.

4. See the "Introduzione" by Federico Roncoroni to *Solus ad solam* (Milan: Mondadori, 1979), 5–56.

5. *Prose*, ed. Roncoroni, cxlvii.

6. G. Battista Nazzaro, "Poetica e immaginario nella scrittura di D'Annunzio," *ES: materiali per il '900* 12/13 (1980):63, 71.

7. Mutterle, *Gabriele D'Annunzio*, 167.

8. For the dates, writing, and rewriting of this material, see *Prose*, ed. Roncoroni, 469–77, 485–86, 509–10.

9. *Le dit du sourd et muet* and *Teneo te Africa* were both published in 1936.

Chapter Seven

1. Gibellini, *Logos e mythos,* 128.
2. Anna Maria Andreoli, *Gabriele D'Annunzio* (Florence: La Nuova Italia, 1984), 3.

Selected Bibliography

PRIMARY SOURCES

Complete Works

Opera omnia. Milan: Mondadori, 1927–1936. 49 vols.
Tutte le opere. Milan: Mondadori, 1939–1950. 9 vols.

Notebooks and Posthumous Collections

Roma senza lupa: cronache mondane, 1884–1888. Edited by A. Baldini and
   P. P. Trompeo. Milan: Domus, 1948.
Taccuini. Milan: Mondadori, 1965.
Altri taccuini. Milan: Mondadori, 1976.
Favole mondane. Edited by Federico Roncoroni. Milan: Garzanti, 1981.
Lettere a Giselda Zucconi. Pescara: Centro nazionale di studi dannunziani,
   1985.

Annotated Collections

Poesie. Edited by Federico Roncoroni. Milan: Garzanti, 1978.
Prose. Edited by Federico Roncoroni. Milan: Garzanti, 1983.
Versi d'amore e di gloria. Edited by Annamaria Andreoli and Niva Lorenzini.
   Milan: Mondadori, 1982–84. 2 vols.

SECONDARY SOURCES

Alatri, Paolo. *D'Annunzio.* Turin: UTET, 1983. The most complete
   biography to date, with reliable information on the works as well.
Bàrberi Squarotti, Giorgio. *Invito alla lettura di Gabriele D'Annunzio.*
   Milan: Mursia, 1982. Brief critical guide to the works.
Caraccio, Armand. *D'Annunzio dramaturge.* Grenoble: Presses Universitaires
   de France. 1950. For the complete theater.
Chiara, Piero. *Vita di Gabriele D'Annunzio.* Milan: Mondadori, 1978.
   Sprightly biography by a popular writer.

De Michelis, Eurialo. *Tutto D'Annunzio*. Milan: Feltrinelli, 1960. Exhaustive guide to all the works.

Goudet, Jacques. *D'Annunzio romanziere*. Florence: Olschki, 1976. Psychoanalytic readings of the novels.

Guglielminetti, Marziano. *Struttura e sintassi del romanzo italiano del primo Novecento*. Milan: Silva, 1964. Extremely interesting "grammatical" approach to the novels.

Jullian, Philippe. *D'Annunzio*. Translated by Stephen Hardman. New York: Viking, 1973 (in French [Paris: Fayard, 1971]). Sensationalist and not always reliable, but very readable.

Ledeen, Michael A. *The First Duce: D'Annunzio at Fiume*. Baltimore: Johns Hopkins University Press, 1977. Careful study of the Fiume adventure.

Lelièvre, Renée. *Le Théâtre dramatique italien en France 1855–1940*. Paris: Armand Colin, 1959. Abundantly documented.

Mariano, Emilio. *Sentimento del vivere ovvero Gabriele D'Annunzio*. Milan: Mondadori, 1962. By the dean of Italian D'Annunzio scholars.

Mazzarella, Arturo. *Il piacere e la morte*. Naples: Liguori, 1983. On the early novels.

Mutterle, Anco Marzio. *Gabriele D'Annunzio: Introduzione e guida allo studio dell'opera dannunziana*. Florence: Le Monnier, 1982. Reliable and intelligent brief guide.

Petronio, Giuseppe. *D'Annunzio*. Palermo: Palumbo, 1977. History of D'Annunzio's reception with an anthology.

Raimondi, Ezio. *Il silenzio della Gorgone*. Bologna: Zanichelli, 1980. By one of the shapers of current thinking about D'Annunzio.

Rhodes, Anthony. *The Poet as Superman: A life of Gabriele D'Annunzio*. London, 1959. Readable biography.

Ricciardi, Mario. *Coscienza e struttura nella prosa di D'Annunzio*. Turin: Giappichelli, 1970. Complex, stimulating study of the prose.

Scarano Lugnani, Emanuella. "Gabriele D'Annunzio." *La letteratura italiana storia e testi*. Edited by Carlo Muscetta. 9,1. *Il Novecento* (Bari: Laterza, 1976), 121–225. Intelligent brief guide to most of the works.

Tessari, Roberto. *Il mito della macchina nella letteratura italiana del primo Novecento*. Milan: Mursia, 1973. D'Annunzio and the dawning industrial age.

Weaver, William. *Duse: A Biography*. New York, 1984. Well-informed study of D'Annunzio's famous companion.

Index

133